THE SERIAL VERB FORMATION IN THE DRAVIDIAN LANGUAGES

MLBD SERIES IN LINGUISTICS

General Editor
DHANESH JAIN

Volume IV

THE SERIAL VERB FORMATION IN THE DRAVIDIAN LANGUAGES

SANFORD B. STEEVER

MOTILAL BANARSIDASS
Delhi Varanasi Patna
Bangalore Madras

First Edition: Delhi, 1988

MOTILAL BANARSIDASS
Bungalow Road, Jawahar Nagar, Delhi 110 007
Branches
Chowk, Varanasi 221 001
Ashok Rajpath, Patna 800 004
24, Race Course Road, Bangalore 560 001
120 Royapettah High Road, Madras 600 004

ISBN: 81-208-0378-7

PRINTED IN INDIA
BY JAINENDRA PRAKASH JAIN AT SHRI JAINENDRA PRESS, A-45 NARAINA INDUSTRIAL AREA, PHASE I, NEW DELHI 110 028 AND PUBLISHED BY NARENDRA PRAKASH JAIN FOR MOTILAL BANARSIDASS, DELHI 110 007

PREFACE

THIS book explores the grammar of the Serial Verb Formation in the Dravidian languages to discover how the interaction of morphology and syntax is mediated by the grammatical property of finiteness. The roots of this study lie within two separate fields of linguistic endeavor: generative morphology, and comparative Dravidian syntax. The two of them converge in the single phenomenon of finiteness, a syntactic property that is morphologically interpreted with the help of agreement rules. Finiteness is derived directly from a syntactic relation that holds between certain constructions and their heads, and proves to be an essential ingredient of the Dravidian sentence. It specifically plays a crucial role in the Serial Verb Formation, which actually embraces a set of structures whose existence in Dravidian has not been recognized hitherto. The analysis of these structures therefore promises to cast new light on the functions of finiteness in the creation of the sentence and its component parts. Accordingly, we seek to establish the existence of the Serial Verb Formation, to explain its inherent properties in terms of the rules that generate it, and to demonstrate how ingeniously it uses finiteness to co-ordinate morphology and syntax in the Dravidian sentence.

Generative grammar tends to view morphology as something of a poor relation, one whose claims to legitimacy and the attentions of scholars seem always to give way to those of syntax. Although there has been significant work in generative morphology, its progress still lags far behind the achievements of syntax. Despite the fact that morphology often encodes information that is syntactic in nature, it cannot readily be reduced to a purely interpretive system. It is an autonomous component of grammar whose constitutive rules obey their own internal logic, and do not necessarily reflect syntactic concepts such as dependency and constituency in any direct way. I suspect that due to the stigma of association with American descriptive linguistics, the study of morphology lost much of its appeal and impetus during the polemical fulminations of generative grammar during the 1960s. What remained of it was partitioned between phonology and syntax. Yet, if morphology and syntax are indeed autonomous components they must interact within the all-encompassing grammatical system of which they are two parts.

Morphology and syntax influence one another most frequently and directly at the level of surface structure. Output constraints, filters, and surface structure formation rules, all of which purport to govern at least in part the well-formedness of surface structures, often include morphological parameters which syntactic rules must obey. A clear example of a morphological constraint on syntax is that one cannot pronounce a form which the lexicon fails to provide with the appropriate morphology. Therefore no syntactic rule may apply to make a word assume a morphology it does not possess. For example, no rule of English may apply so as to place a demonstrative pronoun in a grammatical context that requires the genitive case, e.g. the poss-*ing* construction, a possessor NP: demonstratives lack a genitive case in English (but not in German or Kannaḍa). Certain English verbs such as *allege* have only passive morphology, and must undergo Passivization. Tamil Relative Clause Formation may not extract a noun from a relative clause so that it strands a bound postposition (Steever 1981, Chapter VII). No rule of Tamil, such as Clefting (p. 16), may displace an imperative or hortative verb form into a context that requires a non-finite form: these speech-act forms lack non-finite morphology altogether. Although early work on the lexicon (Seuren 1969), the theory of exceptions (Lakoff 1970), and surface structure constraints (Perlmutter 1971) drew attention to the role of morphological constraints on syntax, it has not been vigorously pursued.

Comparative Dravidian syntax displays the opposite bias: while it has made great strides in phonology, morphology, and lexicon, it has neglected syntax since Bloch's (1946) *Structure grammaticale des langues dravidiennes*. Intense concentration on morphology at the expense of syntax is understandable in the study of these languages. First of all, most Dravidian languages have just two parts of speech: nouns and verbs. Their elaborate inflectional morphology encodes grammatical information which in other languages might well be encoded through syntactic means. Second, the Dravidian languages lack by and large those parts of speech which generative grammarians have so profitably exploited elsewhere in the study of syntax: conjunctions, complementizers, and adverbs. The results of these studies cannot be directly applied to the analysis of Dravidian syntax without the risk of severe distortion. Finally, the native grammatical traditions of India concentrate on the analysis of words: they seek, in modern parlance, to generate well-formed words, not sentences. The pre-generative European grammarians who first undertook the comparative grammar of the Dravidian languages naturally sympathized with this mode of analysis, and tended to ignore syntax.

In the attempt to combine these different concerns, our research begins where Bloch's stopped: at the threshold between the simple and the complex sentence. As an essential ingredient of the Dravidian sentence, finiteness must be regulated in the composition of simple and complex sentences alike. The distribution of finite predicates in the Dravidian sentence, no matter how internally complex, is severely limited: there can be only one in a sentence, and it must appear in the root clause (Chapter I). This restriction on the distribution of finite predicates throws the entire burden of forming complex sentences on the non-finite verb forms of the language.

There are several sets of principled exceptions to this rule, which help to circumvent certain problems which the use of non-finite verb forms entails but cannot solve. These exceptions permit the use of multiple finite predicates in the Dravidian sentence, and are introduced one by one in Chapter II. The Serial Verb Formation is in effect the last in this series of exceptions to the rule that governs the distribution of finite predicates.

The Serial Verb Formation properly includes a set of structures in which two or more finite verb forms co-occur, marking agreement among themselves. Agreement is used here to delineate the syntactic relation between certain verbal constructions and their heads, and differs markedly from its better-known use to mark the subject-predicate relation in the root clause of the sentence. The general features of the Serial Verb Formation are formulated by means of deduction at the beginning of Chapter III. However, since the presence of this set of structures has not been generally recognized in Dravidian, the book must justify its existence and confirm the predictions about its structure with the use of empirical evidence. Accordingly, Chapters III-VI introduce relevant examples from fifteen daughter languages, with one chapter dedicated to each of the four primary subgroups. The Dravidian specialist who doubts the existence of this construction and the general linguist who questions the introduction of so much data may wish to read the first section of Chapter VII first, and then return to the catalogue of forms in the four previous chapters. Chapter VII confirms by induction the predictions made by deduction in Chapter III about the grammar of the Serial Verb Formation. Once that is done, the rule that governs the distribution of finite predicates in the Dravidian sentence is re-formulated to accommodate the Serial Verb Formation, and to integrate it into comparative Dravidian syntax.

Some works of comparative grammar may burst forth fully formed from virtual nothingness, but this is not one of them. It is indebted to the work of many scholars in the fields of general linguistics, Indology, comparative Dravidian grammar, and the individual Dravidian languages. I hope to recognize here all those who have directly contributed to this work through their scholarship and generosity: in Hyderabad: C. Ramarao, Lakshmi Bai, B. Ramakrishna Reddy; in Pune: Peri Bhaskararao, Susie Andres; in Delhi: K. V. Subbarao, Anjani K. Sinha; in Madurai: M. Shanmugam Pillai; in Mysore: D. P. Pattanayak, Francis Ekka, G. Sambasiva Rao, M.B. Ganesh, Thomas and Mary Fogarty; and outside India: Franklin Southworth, Murray B. Emeneau, and Thomas Burrow. Four scholars should be singled out: K. Paramasivam who guided my Tamil Studies in Chicago and Madurai, and whose introduction to the concept of *muṟṟeccam* set this work in motion; N. Bh. Krishnamurti whose expertise in comparative Dravidian grammar and personal interest encouraged me to include all of Dravidian in my research; E. Annamalai who, as Acting Director of the Central Institute of Indian Languages, provided me with an ideal setting

CONVENTIONS

NO ATTEMPT is made here to alter the transcription systems of the various sources, even though examples from a single language may be recorded in two or more competing systems. For example, the transcriptions of Malto vary from one author to the next so that Droese (1884) uses one system and Mahapatra (1979) another. Similarly, no steps are taken to homogenize the diglossic variants of the major literary languages. Examples from literary Tamil (*centamiẓ*) are represented according to Paramasivam's (1979) transcription which follows the *Tamil lexicon* except in its use of *-ẓ-* to represent the retroflex approximant. Examples from colloquial Tamil (*koṭuntamiẓ*) are transliterated directly from their sources following this same transcription, but without "regularizing" the phonology and morphology, e.g. without replacing the colloquial past tense marker *-cc-* with its non-palatalized literary counterpart *-tt-*.

Boundary markers are introduced into the examples in an approximate fashion. Portmanteau morphs are not segmented. No systematic importance attaches to these conventions. Morpheme-by-morpheme glosses accompany the examples: the labels used in the glosses are meant as aids for reading, not as strict morphological analyses.

Dravidian etyma are numbered according to the system provided in *A Dravidian Etymological Dictionary, 2nd edition*, and are identified with the abbreviation *DEDR*. The notatian * has two distinct uses. It accompanies reconstructed forms in historical analysis; but, in a synchronic analysis, it marks a non-occurring or unacceptable form. The context makes it clear in any case which interpretation is meant. The notations used in Word-Formation Rules are ennumerated in Note 6 to Chapter Three.

The following abbreviations represent transformational rules used in the derivations presented in charts:

AC	Auxiliary Contraction
AT	Affix-Truncation
AVD	Auxiliary Verb Deletion
ND	Nasal Degemination
P	Palatalization
VD	Vowel Dissimilation
dna	(rule) does not apply.

The following abbreviations are used in the glosses of the examples:

abl	ablative case

acc	accusative case
adnp	adnominal participle
advs	adversative
bvb	bare verb base
cfc	counterfactual conditional
cond	conditional
cnt	contingent tense
cp	conjunctive participle
dat	dative case
emp	emphatic particle
excl	exclusive
f	feminine
fut	future tense
gen	genitive case
h	honorific
hort	hortative
imp	imperative
impf	imperfect(ive)
incl	inclusive
inf	infinitive
instr	instrumental case
int	interrogative marker
loc	locative case
m	masculine
n	neuter
neg	negative
nom	nominative case
npst	non-past tense
obl	oblique
onom	onomatopoeia
p	plural
pcl	particle
perm	permissive
pl	plural (noun)
pres	present tense
prf	perfect (ive)
prt	participle
pst	past tense
rfx	reflexive
s	singular
soc	sociative case
subj	subjunctive
tag	tag-question

te	truncated ending
tp	transition particle
tpe	truncated personal ending
vn	verbal noun
1	first person
2	second person
3	third person
1pin	first person plural inclusive
1pex	first person plural exclusive
Xsub	subject suffix
Xobj	object suffix

The symbols # and ? used in Tables and Charts and in some parts of the text denote the following:

#	word boundary
?	glottal stop

CONTENTS

LIST OF TABLES

LIST OF CHARTS

Chapter One

FINITENESS AND THE DRAVIDIAN SENTENCE

1. INTRODUCTION

STUDENTS of comparative Dravidian grammar must devote a portion of their research to studying the grammars of the individual languages that make up the Dravidian family.[1] The ground there is so fertile and unexplored that comparison of these grammars can lead them to discover that what appears at first sight to be an anomaly may prove on further inspection to be a common expression that fully conforms to the grammatical system of the language. One such case is the SERIAL VERB FORMATION, a construction in which two or more finite verb forms occur together, marking agreement among themselves.[2] The presence of the serial verb in the Dravidian family may be considered surprising, even perplexing, since it is commonly assumed that the rules of Dravidian syntax limit the number of finite predicates in any sentence to a maximum of one. Evidence presented here reveals, however, that the serial verb is not an oddity to be banished to the obscurity of a footnote, but rather an integral and characteristic parts of Dravidian verb morphology. Fifteen of the daughter languages, representing the four major subgroups, are shown to possess serial verbs in a limited number of recurring patterns, to differ from languages without them by means of simple rules, and to support their reconstruction to Proto-Dravidian. Thus, despite the severe restrictions placed on the distribution of finite predicates in the Dravidian sentence, the serial verb emerges from this study as a lively, integral part of Dravidian grammar.

The first chapter lays the foundation for the analysis of the serial verb: it concentrates on the close relation between finiteness and sentence structure. A rule is proposed that accurately predicts the number and position of finite predicates in the Dravidian sentence. The second chapter continues to examine this relation: it introduces several principled exceptions to this rule, and refines it through successive approximations. The serial verb appears as the last stage in this series of exceptions and revisions. Before the serial verb can be accommodated in a further revision of the rule that governs the distribution of finite predicates, its grammatical properties must be explored. Each of the next four chapters presents a catalogue and analysis of the serial verb as it appears in one of the four subgroups. The last chapter integrates the serial verb into Dravidian grammar: the rule that governs the distribution of finite predicates is revised to make provision for the serial verb. The serial verb is reconstructed to Proto-Dravidian, and its subsequent loss or retention in the development of the individual daughter languages is described with the help of simple rules.

2. FINITENESS AS A GRAMMATICAL PROPERTY

A rapid inspection of the grammars of the Dravidian languages reveals that the term finiteness occurs repeatedly in the grammatical description of predicates, particularly in chapters on verb morphology. But despite the frequency with which it appears, it has little more than a heuristic value: it is usually left undefined, and is applied as an unanalyzed label to a specified set of verb forms. Finiteness is variously treated in these grammars as though it were a term that pertained to morphology, syntax, or both. According to the morphological characterization, which is the most common, finiteness is a term in the opposition of finite versus non-finite, and is applied solely to verbs. A predicate is finite or not depending as it is a verb that is inflected for tense and subject-verb agreement, or not.[3] According to the syntactic characterization, on the other hand, finiteness is a property of sentence structure: certain syntactic rules identify a specially designated position in the constituent structure of a sentence where only finite predicates may occur. A predicate is finite or not depending as it occurs in that specially designated position or not.[4] Based as they are on different criteria, these two definitions naturally make different claims about the sorts of linguistic objects that may properly be said to be finite. According to the first, only those predicates that are morphologically verbs can ever be finite; according to the second, only those predicates with a certain syntactic distribution are finite.

The morphological and syntactic treatments of finiteness can be reconciled despite the different claims they make: finiteness may be characterized as a syntactic property of predicates that is morphologically interpreted. This synthesis accords syntax the pivotal role in the definition, for which both formal and substantive arguments may be advanced. While morphology establishes only necessary conditions for a predicate to be finite, syntax establishes both necessary and sufficient conditions. Certain verb forms provide us with empirical evidence in favor of the primacy of syntax, as well. A number of modal auxiliary verbs such as Tamil *kūṭāu* 'should not' and Kannaḍa *bēku* 'must' are apparent counter-examples to the morphological definition of the finite predicate as a verb that marks tense and subject-verb agreement. Although these modals occur in exactly the same environments as garden-variety finite verbs do, they do not overtly mark tense or subject-verb agreement. Moreover, these modals lack non-finite counterparts, and so cannot in one sense be defined as finite since they fail to contrast with any corresponding non-finite forms. Similar arguments may be constructed on the basis of certain verb forms that are used to convey speech-acts, including the imperative, the optative, the hortative, e.g. Tamil *-lām*, Kannaḍa *-ōṇa*, and the permissive, e.g. Tamil *-aṭṭum*, Kannaḍa *-ali*. These forms lack overt markings for tense and subject-verb agreement,[5] and do not morphologically contrast with non-finite forms.[6] These two sets of counter-examples do not drastically compromise the morphological definition of finiteness, for they can be readily accommodated with the help of a subsidiary theory of defective morphology that analyzes them as defective verbs which covertly encode their finiteness and lack non-finite counterparts. As convenient as this tactic may seem, the decision to label these predicates as finite ultimately rests on the syntactic observation that they occur in the very same grammatical environment as ordinary finite verbs do.

Predicate nominals raise a serious challenge to the morphological definition of finiteness in the Dravidian languages. Comparison of a wide range of sentences reveals a startling fact: predicate nominals occur in exactly the same grammatical environment as ordinary finite verbs. The syntactic rules that pinpoint the specially designated position in a sentence where finite predicates occur, do not in their operation distinguish between predicate nominals and finite verbs of any sort. Although predicate nominals behave syntactically like finite verbs, they cannot be considered to be finite verbs because, as nouns, they can never mark verbal categories such as tense or mood.[7] Nor can they be treated as modals and imperatives were, that is, as if they were severely defective verbs. Any theory of morphology that identified predicate nominals as defective verbs would, at that level of abstraction, have ceased to be a theory of grammatical forms and categories altogether. The decision to apply the label of finiteness to some predicate squarely rests, not on such morphological criteria as the ability to bear certain verbal inflections, but on such syntactic criteria as the ability to occur in that position in a sentence which is specially designated for finite predicates.[8] Thus, to capture the generalization that finite verbs and predicate nominals have the same grammatical behavior, a syntactic theory of finiteness is required.

3. FINITENESS AND SENTENCE STRUCTURE

Dravidian linguists have long been aware of the central role that finite predicates play in the construction of the Dravidian sentence. Bishop Caldwell (1976: 490) describes the relation between finiteness and sentence structure in an observation that is based on Tamil specifically, and comparative Dravidian grammar generally.

> In every sentence there is but one finite verb, which is the last word in the sentence, and the seat of government; and all the verbs which express subordinate actions of circumstance, whether antecedent or contemporaneous,

> assume an indeterminate, continuative character, as verbal participles or gerundials, without the need of conjunctions or copulatives of any kind; so that the sense (and more or less the time also) waits in suspense for the authoritative decision of the final governing verb . . . Tamil grammarians class them, together with infinitives and subjunctives, as *vinei echcham*, verb defects, or verbal complements—i.e., words which require a verb to complete the sense.

In his grammar of Kannaḍa, Spencer (1985: 4) records much the same observation about the composition of Kannaḍa sentences : '. . . a Kanarese sentence rarely tolerates more than one finite verb. One verb only in the sentence will be finite in form. Verbs which, in English, would be co-ordinate with it are put in the form of the past participle.' And Winfield (1928 : 132), in his grammar of Kūi, notes the constant use of conjunctional participles in the construction of complex sentences to avoid more than one finite verb.

> The conjunctional participles, affirmative and negative, are used in order to avoid the constant repetition of finite verbs in short simple sentences. Instead of using a finite verb in the indicative followed by the conjunction *enga, and,* the significance of the verb's action is carried over from one clause into the next and connected with it by using the conjunctional participle . . . .

From these and similar passages may be extracted the constraint that no Dravidian sentence may have more than one finite verb, which must occur at the extreme right end of the sentence. Since these three authors rely on a morphological definition of finiteness, their observations on the relation between finiteness and sentence structure are inexact. They establish only an upper limit on the number of finite verb forms that may appear in the Dravidian sentence, thereby allowing for the possibility of sentences without any finite verb form at all. This incorrectly predicts the existence of sentences whose predicates are all non-finite verb forms.[9] It does, however, leave open the possibility of sentences whose predicate is a predicate nominal. Even so, it fails to recognize that predicate nominals are themselves finite predicates, and could lead one to conclude, counter-factually, that some Dravidian sentences contain both a finite verb form and a predicate nominal.[10] None of these problems will arise below when we formulate the constraint on finiteness and sentence structure in terms of the syntactic definition of finiteness, and speak of finite predicates, not verbs.

The use of modern linguistic concepts can further help us to refine our statements on the distribution of the finite predicate in the Dravidian sentence. The single finite predicate stands at the extreme right boundary of the sentence, commands all other predicates, and is itself commanded by none of them.[11] That is, it occurs in the root clause of the surface constituent structure of the sentence. Any rule that uniquely identifies the predicate in the root clause of the sentence, automatically identifies the specially designated position where only finite predicates may appear. The subsequent application of morphological rules will then interpret the syntactic property of finiteness according to the lexical category and morphological status of the predicate that occupies the specially designated position.[12] The sentence is thus the domain of the property of finiteness in the grammar of the Dravidian languages.

A First Approximation

The rule that governs the distribution of finite predicates in the Dravidian sentence is stated below in a first approximation to its final form. A series of exceptions to this rule, including the serial verb, is introduced as we test its descriptive capacity, and it is successively refined to accommodate them.

(1) RULE FOR THE DISTRIBUTION OF FINITE PREDICATES

(a) The Dravidian sentence has exactly one finite predicate.

(b) The finite predicate appears in the root clause of the surface constituent structure of the sentence: it stand at the extreme right boundary of the sentence, commands all other predicates, and is itself commanded by none.[13]

(c) Consequently, all other predicates in the sentence are non-finite.

The heart of this rule is expressed in sections (1)a and (1)b; section (1)c follows as a straightforward inference from them. The first section fixes the number of finite predicates in the Dravidian sentence at one, while the second locates its exact position in the constituent structure. But before we can test the descriptive adequacy of this rule, we must first equip ourselves with some background information about Dravidian morphology and syntax.

4. A SKETCH OF DRAVIDIAN MORPHOLOGY

Dravidian morphology is transparent, agglutinating, and predominantly suffixal. The order of elements in a word is: lexical root, derivational suffix, and inflectional suffix. The majority of the Dravidian languages distinguish just two parts of speech according to their morphology: noun and verb, both of which may occur in simple and compound form. Although many other parts of speech are ennumerated in some grammars, they can easily he resolved into various combinations of nouns and verbs.[14] In addition to these two basic parts of speech, the Dravidian languages also possess a small set of morphemes that encode meanings such as quantification and emphasis in post-clitic particles. Their role in the composition of complex sentences is discussed in next chapter.

Nouns are typically inflected for categories such as case, person, number, and gender. The common Dravidian case system includes eight cases: nominative, accusative, dative, genitive instrumental, locative, and ablative.[15] These eight are regularly supplemented by postpositions, derived from independent noun or non-finite verbs. The categories of person and number are marked not only in pronouns, but also, in certain languages, in predicate nominals. In Old Tamil, for example, predicate nominals are inflected to agree with their subjects, e.g. in *nām nāṭṭ-ōm* 'we$_1$ (are) countrymen$_2$'-*ōm* marks agreement with the first person plural subject. Two numbers are distinguished: singular and plural. Dravidian gender distinguishes animate and inanimate nouns according to the natural gender of their referents, not on the basis of 'grammatical' or conventionally ascribed gender. Animate nouns may be further classified as honorific, masculine, or feminine. The deictic noun **avan* 'that man, he' illustrates succinctly the compound noun in Dravidian: it consists of the nouns **a-* 'that (one)' and *-(*v*)*an* 'man'. Although large compond nouns often appear in our English translations as a sequence of numeral, adjective, and noun, they have the internal structure of a compound noun all the same.

Verbs are inflected, naturally enough, for verbal categories such as tense and mood. Proto-Dravidian has two tenses, past and non-past, and two moods, modal and indicative. A verb is formally finite or not, depending as it is inflected for tense and subject-verb agreement, or not. The crucial role of finite verb forms in the construction of the Dravidian sentence has already been emphasized in the discussion preceding the statement of Rule (1). Suffice it to say here that the finite verb occurs at the very end of the sentence, and so brings it to a close. Dravidian verb morphology recognizes two basic kinds of non-finite verb form: both of them by definition combine with a following word, and so do not close the sentence. The first kind includes all those verb forms that combine with a following noun to form relative clauses and other noun complements. They are known in traditional Tamil grammar as *peyareccam*, or 'verbs that anticipate a following noun,' and include the adnominal, or relative participles.[16] The second kind includes all those verb forms that combine with a following verb to form compound verbs or complex sentences. Known in traditional Tamil grammar as *viṉaiyeccam*, or 'verbs that anticipate a following verb', they include the infinitive, the conjunctive participle, and the conditional. Tamil commentators observe that a non-finite verb form properly combines with the lexical root of the following word, not an inflected form, so that this combinatoric process may reapply indefinitely and recursively. In both kinds, the non-finite verb form and the word it combines with may be adjacent or separated by intervening material. The Dravidian languages rely on a rich set of compound verbs to extend the somewhat limited resources of the set of simple verb forms. Lexical compound verbs supplement the lexicon by providing a complex morphosyntactic vehicle for those combinations of lexical meanings that are not encoded in any single verb root of the language. For example, the Tamil lexical compound verb *aẓaittuk koṇṭu vara* 'invite' consists of the conjunctive participles of *aẓaikka* 'call', *koḷḷa* 'hold', and an inflected form of *vara* 'come'. Auxiliary compound verbs provide a complex morphosyntactic vehicle for those verbal categories that are not encoded in any simple verb inflection of the language, e.g. perfect tense, benefactive voice. In the spoken Kannaḍa example, *nānu bandu iddīni* 'I_1 $have_3$ $come_2$' the auxiliary verb *iddīni* 'I am' signals present perfect tense.

Conspicuous in their absence from the parts of speech in Dravidian are those word-classes that acquaintance with more familiar languages might lead us to believe are indispensible to the formation of complex sentences: adverbs (*since*, *during*), conjunctions (*and*, *but*), and complementizers(*that*, *for . . . to*). Although clitics play a small role, the construction of complex sentences must rely on the two existing parts of speech to carry out those functions that are typically ascribed to these other "missing" parts of speech. Since the theory of case describes the grammatical relation between a predicate and its arguments within a single clause, and not across clauses, case-marking does not figure in the formation of complex sentences.[17] Virtually all of the burden of creating complex sentences falls on non-finite verb forms.

For details about the morphology of particular laguages, the reader should refer to the grammars of individual languages and to handbooks of comparative grammar, e.g. Bloch (1946), P.S. Subrahmanyam (1971), S.V. Shanmugam (1971), Andronov (1970), Zvelebil (1977). These grammars show us how the morphology of the individual daughter languages has developed—often deviated—from the common Dravidian norm. A simple present tense form has evolved in Tamil so that the language now possesses a system of three simple tense forms. In Kannaḍa the distinction between the instrumental and ablative cases has been neutralized in favor of what historically was the ablative.

5. A SKETCH OF DRAVIDIAN SYNTAX

The dominant word-order in Dravidian is subject-object-verb (SOV). In Dravidian, as in other rigid SOV languages, this basic word-order implies a number of harmonic correlations: genitives precede the nouns they modify main verbs precede auxiliaries, and complements precede their matrix clauses. Although the explicit noun morphology permits some freedom of variation in word-order within a clause, the verb remains at the extreme right end of its clause,

Subject-predicate agreement follows a nominative-accusative pattern, not an ergative-absolutive one.

Simple Sentences

The Dravidian simple sentence consists of a subject and a predicate. The subject is a noun-phrase that is inflected for the nominative or, in certain circumstances, the dative case.[18] The application of Rule (1) to a simple sentence marks the predicate as finite, so the predicate is either a finite verb or a predicate nominal. From the various combinations of subject and predicate, four basic sentence patterns emerge: (1) nominative subject and predicate nominal; (2) nominative subject and finite verb; (3) dative subject and predicate nominal; and (4) dative subject and finite verb. Predicate nominals themselves appear in the nominative case, which is the least marked of all the cases. No copula is required in sentences with predicate nominals. Each of these four basic patterns is illustrated below with Tamil examples.

(2) TAMIL

(a) *avar* *āciriyar.*
he-h-nom teacher-nom
'He (is a) teacher.'

(b) *avar* *va-nt-ār.*
he-h-nom come-pst-3sh
'He came.'

(c) *avar-ukku oru makaṉ.*
he-h-dat one son-non
'He (has) a son.'

(d) *avar-ukku kōpam* *va-nt-atu.*
he-h-dat anger-nom com-pst-3sn
'He got angry.'

Sentence (2)a consists of the nominative subject *avar* 'he' and the predicate nominal *āciriyar* 'teacher'. While sentence (2)b also has the nominative subject *avar* 'he', its predicate is the finite verb *vantār* 'he came'. Sentence (2)c consists of the dative subject *avarukku* 'to him' and the predicate nominal *oru makaṉ* 'a son'. Finally, sentence (2)d consists of the dative subject *avarukku* 'to him' and the finite verb *vantatu* 'it come'. As has been noted above, some Dravidian languages possess a variation on the first pattern, in which the predicate nominal is inflected to agree with the subject. Though Modern Tamil lacks this variant, Old Tamil has it.

(3) OLD TAMIL

nām *nāṭṭ-ōm.*
we-nom country-1p
'We (are) countrymen.'

Rule (1) correctly ascribes the property of finiteness to the predicate in each of these five examples.

These four basic sentence patterns serve as templates through which other syntactic structures in the language are fitted. Tamil has a rule of CLEFTING which postposes a noun-phrase to the right of the clause-final finite verb. Simultaneously, the finite verb becomes a verbal noun, and the oblique case marking on the postposed noun-phrase, if any, is optionally deleted. Clefting transforms sentence (4)a into (4)b.

(4) TAMIL

(a) *nāṉ* *maturai-(y)il* *piṟa-nt-ēṉ.*
I-nom Maduri-loc be born-pst-1s
'I was born in Madurai.'

(b) *nāṉ* *piṟa-nt-atu* *maturai.*
I-nom be born-pst-vn-nom Madurai-nom
'Where I was born is Madurai.'

The transformed sentence (4)b clearly conforms to the first sentence pattern introduced above, and illustrated in (2)a: the new subject *piṟantatu* 'where X was born' is inflected for the nominative case, as is the new predicate nominal *maturai* 'Madurai'. Finiteness thus seems to be a necessary ingredient for the well-formedness of a sentence at the level of surface structure.

Inspection of other Dravidian languages provides us with similar patterns of simple sentences, as the following Kannaḍa and Konḍa examples show.

(5) KANNAḌA

(a) *avaru* *adhyāpakaru.*
he-h-nom teacher-nom
'He (is a) teacher.'

(b) *avaru* *ba-nd-aru.*
he-h-nom come-pst-3sh
'He came.'

(c) *avar-ige* *obba* *maga.*
he-h-dat one-m son-nom
'He (has) a son.'

(d) *avar-ige* *tamiḷu* *bar at-te.*
he-h-dat Tamil-nom come-npst-3sn
'He knows Tamil.'

(6) KONḌA

(a) *māp* *sēna dūram-ti*
we-nom very distance-abl
lōku
people-nom
'We (are) people from far away.'

(b) *bānza-raza*
barren king-nom
suṟ-t-an.
see-pst-3sm
'The barren king saw.'

(c) *aya* *guruy-eng* *budi.*
that guru-dat wisdom
'That guru (has) wisdom.'

(d) *lōk-aŋ* *kōpam*
man-dat anger-nom
va-n-ad.
come-pst-3sn
'The man gets angry.'

A brief comparison of these examples with their Tamil counterparts above reveals a point-by-point correspondance in their fundamental syntactic structure.

Further examples from the Central Dravidian languages Parji and Kolami and the North Dravidian languages Malto and Kuṛux confirm the robust presence of these four basic patterns throughout the Dravidian family. For brevity's sake, only two patterns from each of the languages are presented: the Parji and Malto examples have predicate nominals, while the Kolami and Kuṛux examples have finite verbs.

(7) PARJI

(a) *āṭ cendan-ed gõvar.*
market go-vn-nom fool-nom
'The man who goes to the market (is) a fool.'

(b) *ōnuŋ sat-jan cind-ul.*
he-dat seven people son-pl-nom
'He (has) seven sons.'

(8) KOLAMI

(a) *ān var-at-un.*
I-nom come-fut-1s
I will come.'

(b) *māk-uŋ doḍḍe kay-t-in.*
tree-dat fruit-nom bear-pst-3
'The tree bore fruit.'

(9) MALTO

(a) *āh eṅki baya-h.*
he-nom my brother-nom-3sm
'He (is) my brother.'

(b) *sardare-k ēna goṭu gāydu?*
chief-dat how many cow-nom
'How many cows does the chief have?'

(10) KUṚUX

(a) *ēn cigla-n ēr-d-an*
I-nom jackal-acc see-pst-1s
'I saw the jackal.'

(b) *puni-ge naṛi bar-c-a.*
Puni-dat fever-nom come-pst-3sn
'Puni got a fever.'

These sentences conform to the four basic sentence patterns introduced above. Their distribution throughout the entire family buttresses our claim that they represent part of a common Dravidian heritage, and may thus be reconstructed to the proto-language.

Although each of these examples confirms the predictions of Rule (1), none of them fully tests its descriptive copacity because each is a simple sentence with a single predicate.[19] Rule (1) pertains essentially to the structure of complex sentences, of which the simple sentence is but a limiting case. An adequate test of this rule must therefore assess the ability of the rule correctly to predict the structure of complex sentences.

Complex Sentences

It will be recalled from an earlier discussion that non-finite verb forms figure prominently in the formation of complex sentences. Two basic kinds of non-finite verbs may be distinguished on the basis of their combinatoric properties: *viṉaiyeccam*, which combine with a following predicate, and *peyareccam*, which combine with a following nominal expression.[20] The three following sets of examples from Tamil indicate the role that *viṉaiyeccam* play in the construction of complex sentences.

(11) TAMIL

(a) *maẓai* *pey-tu* *veyil* *aṭi-ttu* *vāṉavil*
rain-nom rain-cp sun-nom beat-cp rainbow-nom
tōṉṟ-iy-atu.
appear-pst-3sn
'It rained, the sun shined, and a rainbow appeared.'

(b) *nāṉ* *kumār* *kār* *ōṭṭ-i* *pār-tt-ēṉ.*
I-nom Kumar-nom car-acc drive-cp see-pst-1s
'I saw Kumar driving a car.'

(c) *makaṉai* *pār-ttu* *eṉakku* *mika* *cantōṣam.*
son-acc see-cp I-dat much pleasure-nom
'I am very happy to have seen my son.'

The use of the conjunctive participle (cp), also known as the adverbial participle, is illustrated in these three sentences. Only the third and final conjunct of the co-ordinate sentence in (11)a has a finite predicate, *tōṉṟiyatu* 'it appeared', whereas the two preceding conjuncts have as their predicates the non-finite conjunctive participles *peytu* 'raining' and *aṭittu* 'beating. The conjunctive participle *ōṭṭi* 'driving' marks the subordinate clause in (11) b, while the finite verb *pārtteṉ* 'I saw appears in the root clause, marking the closure of the sentence.[21] In (11) c the conjunctive participle *pārttu* 'seeing' combines, not with a following verb, but with a predicate nominal *cantōṣam* 'pleasure'. It is for this reason that the term *viṉaiyeccam* is henceforth interpreted syntactically as 'a verb that anticipates a following predicate'. In none of these examples may the finite predicate appear in the position occupied by the conjunctive participle, and vice versa. Any such substitution would result in an ungrammatical sentence. This evidence lends support to our formulation of Rule (1).

(12) TAMIL

(a) *kamalā* *pāṭ-a* *carojā* *āṭ-iṉ-āḷ.*
Kamala-nom sing-inf Saroja-nom dance-pst-3sf
'As Kamala sang, Saroja danced.'

(b) *nāṉ* *avaṉai* *var-a* *coṉ-ṉ-ēṉ.*
I-nom he-acc come-inf tell-pst-1s
'I told him to come.'

(c) *teyvattiṉ* *aruḷ* *kiṭai-kka* *kaviñar* *uṇarcciyuṭaṉ*
god-gen grace get-inf poet-nom feeling-soc
pāṭ-in-ār.
sing-pst-3sh
'The poet sang with emotion to obtain God's grace,' or,
'The poet having obtained God's grace, sang with emotion.'

(d) *eṅkē* *pōk-a*?
where go-inf
'Where is one to go?'

These sentences illustrate the use of the infinitive (inf) in the formation of Tamil sentences. Though the infinitive occurs perhaps most often as part of a compound verb, it also helps to form complex sentences. Examples (12)a and c illustrate the infinitive of circumstance, while (12)b shows how a verb of ordering governs an infinitival complement. These three examples both conform to and confirm the predictions of Rule (1), but (12) d presents a problem because it contains an infinitive where Rule (1) predicts none should occur.[22] There are three possible explanations for the appearance of the infinitive in this context. First, this example may well be an elliptical utterance whose fully restored form embeds the infinitive under a finite verb form such as the imperative *colluṅkaḷ* 'tell (me)'. Second, and related to the first, is the possibility that in this context the infinitive has the illocutionary force of an indirect speech-act, most probably a queclarative. Verb forms that encode such an illocutionary force tend to be finite, as earlier discussion suggests. Finally, Rule (1) might be re-phrased in terms of markedness relations, so that it is unmarked for a finite predicate to occur in the specially designated position for finite predicates, and unmarked for non-finite predicates to occur elsewhere. This would permit the possibility of the infinitive, the least marked verb form in Tamil, to appear in the position designated for finite predicates, although its appearance there would be marked.[23] I suspect that all three explanations will contribute to the ultimate solution of this problem.

(13) TAMIL

(a) *makaṉ* *poy* *conn-āl* *ammā* *aṭi-pp-āl.*
son-nom lie tell-cond mother-nom beat-fut-3sf
'If the son lies, his mother will beat him.'

(b) *nān* *coṉṉ-āl* *avaṉ* *kēṭṭ-āl* *tāṉē* !
I-nom say-cond he-nom hear-cond indeed
'If only he listened when I spoke !

These two examples introduce the conditional (cond), a non-finite verb form that appears in the protasis of a conditional proposition and instantiates the logical operator of material implication. Since the conditional verb precedes the finite verb in (13)a, the sentence as a whole conforms to Rule (1). Sentence (13)b does not as readily yield to analysis, however, because the conditional *kēṭṭāl* 'if X listens' seems to occupy a position that Rule (1) reserves only for finite predicates. Two possible solutions present themselves. First, such a sentence may be elliptical, and in its fuller form possess a finite predicate such as the predicate nominal *nallatu* 'good thing'. This addition to (13) b gives rise to an interpretation that adequately represents its use to express a wish, viz. 'it would be a good thing if he listens when I speak'. The second solution has much in common with the first. Instead of treating the form *tāṉē* 'indeed', which always appears in this construction, as a sequence of two clitic particles, we might instead analyze it as a combination of a predicate nominal *tāṉ* meaning 'appropriateness, exactness' and the emphatic particle-*ē* 'even'. This done, the sentence may be adequately interpreted to mean 'it is appropriate for him to listen when I speak'. Note that like the infinitive in (12)d, the conditional in (13)b encodes an illocutionary force, akin to a desiderative, and thereby expresses an indirect speech-act. Both solutions, whichever we choose, give rise to a "normalized" form whose gross structure conforms to Rule (1). Although examples are omitted here, both the negative verbal participle in *-āmal* and the negative conditional in *-āviṭṭāl* strictly conform to the syntactic predictions of Rule (1).

The following examples illustrate the use of *peyareccam* in the formation of complex sentences, and introduce the adnominal participle, known also as the adjectival or relative participle. It is a non-finite verb form that serves to form nominal complements by subordinating a clause with a verbal predicate to a head noun.

(14) TAMIL

(a) *nāṉ* *ūrukku* *va-nt-a* *mantiriyai* *canti-pp-ēṉ*
I-nom town-dat come-pst-adnp minister-acc meet-fut-1s
'I shall meet the minister who came to town.'

(b) *nāṉ* *mantiri* *va-nt-a* *ceyti* *kēṭ-t-ēṉ.*
I-nom minister-nom come-pst-adnp news hear-pst-1s
'I heard the news that the minister came.'

(c) *mantiri* *va-nt-a* *pōtu* *paraparappu* *iru-nt-atu.*
minister-nom come-pst-adnp time hub bub-nom be-pst-3sn
'There was a hub-bub when the minister came.'

Since the adnominal participle marks tense or negation, but not subject-verb agreement, it is morphologically non-finite. It is crucial to the formation of relative clauses as in (14) a where the participle *vanta* 'which came' combines with the following head noun *mantiri* 'minister' to form the kernel of the relative clause. It appears in other structures, as well. In (14)b the participle *vanta* combines with the head noun *ceyti* 'news' to create a factive nominal complement. In (14)c the participle *vanta* combines with the head noun *pōtu* 'time, when' to create a so-called adverbial clause. The construction of these sentences continues to bear out the predictions of Rule (1) concerning the distribution of finite and non-finite predicates in the Dravidian sentence.

The verbal noun (vn) resembles the adnominal participle in many ways: it marks tense, but not subject-verb agreement, and subordinates the preceding clause to the following. It is probable that the two differ only in that the verbal noun has a pronominal head, which it incorporates, while the adnominal participle has a full lexical head noun.[24]

(15) TAMIL

(a) *mantiri* *va-nt-at-ai* *avaṉ* *pār-tt-āṉ.*
minister-nom come-pst-vn-acc he-nom see-pst-3sm
'He saw that the minister had come.'

(b) *avaṉ* *varu-kiṟ-atu-kku* *muṉ* *nāṉ* *pōy* *viṭuvēṉ.*
he-nom come-pres-vn-dat before I-nom go-cp leave-fut-1s
'Before he comes, I'll go away.'

(c) *mantiri* *eṉakku* *vēlai* *koṭu-tt-av-ar.*
minister-nom I-dat work give-pst-vn-3sh-nom
'The minister is the one who gave me work.'

The verbal noun bears the case-marking imposed upon it by the main clause in which it appear. In (15)a the verbal noun *vantatu* 'that which came' is inflected for the accusative case-marker *-ai* since it is the direct object of the finite verb *pārttāṉ* 'he saw'. In (15)b, on the other hand, the verbal noun *varukiṟatu* 'that which comes' assumes the dative case-marker *-kku* because it combines with the postposition *muṉ* 'before' which governs the dative. Finally, in (15)c the verbal noun *koṭuttavar* 'he who gave' is inflected for the nominative case, and functions as a predicate nominal. All of these examples conform to the guidelines that Rule (1) establishes for the distribution of finite and non-finite predicates in the Dravidian sentence.

The next two sets of examples supplement and support our observations about the use of non-finite verb forms in the construction of complex sentences in the Dravidian languages. The Koṇḍa examples represent the south-central subgroup, the Parji examples the central subgroup. The northern subgroup is omitted here because it has undergone massive syntactic changes which can be noted only in the next chapter.

(16) KONḌA

(a)

or	*nēṇḍ*	*vaz-i*	*darmam*	*kiʔ a*
one	day	come-cp	help	do-imp

'Come for a day, and help us.'

(b)

anasi	*uṇ-ḍeŋ*	*bas-t-an.*
elder brother-nom	eat-inf	sit-pst-3sm

'The older brother sat (down) to eat.'

(c)

embe	*suṛ-tiŋa*	*nāṟu*	*sil-ed.*
where	look-cond	town-nom	not be-pst-3sn

'Wherever they looked, there was no town.'

(d)

ṛū-n-i	*guiḍ-ed*	*soRad.*
plough-fut-adnp	field-loc	go-pst-3sn

'She went to the field that they plough.'

(e)

aya	*bōdel*	*suṛ-t-ika*	*idʔ ed.*
that	woman-nom	see-pst-vn	leave-neg-pst-3sn

'That woman did not leave what she saw alone.'

(17) PARJI

(a)

pokkali	*būta*	*cāj-i*	*ān*	*pan-ḍ-en.*
daytime	all	work-cp	I-nom	tire-pst-1s

'I got tired because I worked all day.'

(b)

atni	*men-uŋ*	*men-uŋ*	*nav*	*mayna*	*errav*	*ge.*
thus	be-inf	be-inf	nine	months	become-pst-3np	indeed

'Nine months passed, as things remained the same.'

(c)

ili	*tōnd-oḍ*	*tapp-ar.*
bear-nom	appear-cond	kill-hort

'If a bear appears, let us kill it.'

(d)

murtal	*cokr-an*	*pott-en*	*iṛki-t-ed.*
old woman-nom	sit-adnp	sack-acc	take-pst-3sm

'He took the sack that the old woman had been sitting on.'

(e)

gōli	*aṛr-ano*	*ām*	*vet-t-om.*
jackal-nom	howl-vn-3sn	we-nom	hear-pst-1p

'We heard the jackal howling.'

Comparison of these examples with the earlier Tamil sentences demonstrates that Rule (1) has the same descriptive power in the south-central and central subgroups as it does in the south subgroup. There is exactly one finite predicate per sentence, and all remaining predicates are non-finite verb forms. The single finite predicate appears at the extreme right boundary of the sentence and commands all other predicates.

An Exception to Precedence Relations

The first principled exception to Rule (1) concerns the proper location of the finite predicate in the left-to-right linear order of the sentence. The clause in (1)b stipulates that the single finite predicate in the Dravidian sentence should occur at the extreme right-hand boundary of the sentence, and that no non-finite predicate should follow it. In light of the following evidence, this stipulation must be revised to accommodate a common sentence pattern in which a non-finite verb form, usually the conjunctive participle, follows the finite predicate. Although this pattern occurs throughout the family, we will limit ourselves to presentation of examples from Tamil and Kannaḍa.

(18) TAMIL

(a) *pāpu avaḷai orumuṟai pār-tt-āṉ nimir-ntu.*
Babu-nom she-acc strangely look-pst-3sm lift-cp
'Babu looked up at her strangely.'

(a') *pāpu avaḷai orumuṟai nimir-ntu pār-tt-āṉ.*
Babu-nom she-acc strangely lift-cp look-pst-3sm
'Babu looked up at her strangely.'

(b) *civa pūjai kūṭa cey-kiṟ-ār, tīṭcai eṭu-ttu koṇ-ṭu.*
Siva puja even do-pres-3sh vow take-cp hold-cp
'He even performs a Siva puja, having taken a vow (to do so).'

(b') *tīṭcai eṭu-ttu koṇ-ṭu civa pūjai kūṭa cey-kiṟ-ār.*
vow take-cp hold-cp Siva puja even do-pres-3sh
'He even performs a Siva puja, having taken a vow (to do so).'

(19) KANNAḌA

(a) *avaḷu mātanāḍ-id-aḷu nagu-tta.*
she-nom speak-pst-3sf laugh-pres-cp
'She spoke laughingly,' i.e., 'She spoke with a laugh.'

(a') *avaḷu nagu-tta mātanāḍ-id-aḷu.*
she-nom laugh-pres-cp speak-pst-3sf
'She spoke with a laugh.'

(b) *amma baredu id-d-āḷe, ninage jarūri*
mother-nom write-pst-cp be-pres-3sf you-dat urgent
kelasa anta.
work-nom say-pres-cp
'Mother wrote, (saying,) "You have urgent work."'

(b') *amma ninage jarūri kelasa*
mother-nom you-dat urgent work-nom
anta baredu id-d-āḷe.
say-pres-cp write-pst-cp be-pres-3sf
'Mother wrote, (saying,) "You have urgent work."'

The first sentence in each of these pairs contains a conjunctive participle which follows the finite predicate, contrary to the predictions of Rule (1). Take (18)a for example. In the first version of this sentence, (18)a, the conjunctive participle *nimirntu* 'lifting' unexpectedly follows the finite verb *pārttāṉ* 'he looked', while in the second version, (18)a', it precedes it. The three remaining pairs of sentences present us with the same pattern of alternation. The first member of each pair exhibits the marked order with non-finite verb following finite predicate, while the second member shows the unmarked order by reversing the two. A grammatical rule has been proposed in Steever (1983 : 214, pass.) to account for this alternation: a rule of CONJUNCTIVE PARTICIPLE POSTPOSING is posited to transform the unmarked order into the marked. The rule is a root transformation, is upward-bounded, and is stylistic with no semantic or syntactic consequences beyond a transposition in surface linear order. Even so, the marked order contradicts the predictions of Rule (1) regarding the relative linear order between finite and non-finite predicates.

One solution to this problem holds that Rule (1) applies, not to surface structure, but to shallow structure, before the application of stylistic rules. On this proposal Rule (1) applies before Conjunctive Participle Postposing, and is fully satisfied by sentences with the unmarked order. Another solution is to say that the permutation of the conjunctive participle rightwards over the finite predicate changes nothing but precedence relations, and leaves undisturbed the hierarchical command relations of the unmarked version of the sentence. According to this proposal the finite verb *mātanāḍidaḷu* 'she spoke' commands the conjunctive participle *nagutta* 'laughing', no matter whether it precedes or follows it in (19)a. The stipulation that the finite predicate should command all other predicates would in both instances identify *mātanāḍidaḷu* as the finite predicate. This solution encourages us to interpret Rule (1), not just as one pedestrian rule among many, but as an essential constraint on the well-formedness of surface structure. Some revision may be needed, however. Rule (1) might easily omit all reference to linear order, and rely solely on command relations to identify the unique finite predicate in the sentence. While the rules that construe the left-to-right order of elements in the sentence could draw upon the information contained in command relations, they would nevertheless be distinct from them. There is no pressing need to choose one solution or the other at this juncture. So, at the risk of including too much information in Rule (1), we will continue to specify the linear order of the finite predicate, if only as a heuristic device to help the reader find the finite predicates in the examples that follow.

6. SUMMARY

The formulation of Rule (1) is a first attempt to describe how morphology and syntax interact in the formation of the Dravidian sentence. Finiteness is the nexus of this interaction: it is a syntactic property that is subsequently interpreted in morphological terms. Only one predicate is finite : all remaining predicates must consequently be non-finite. Whereas the finite predicate may be a predicate nominal or a finite verb form, all non-finite predicates are verb forms. Rule (1) is a constraint on the well-formedness of surface structures to which the output of transformational rules must conform. An accommodation was made for the first exception to Rule (1), which deals with precedence relations. Evidence from a variety of Dravidian languages in three of the four major subgroups largely confirms the descriptive adequacy of Rule (1).

Chapter Two

MULTIPLE FINITE PREDICATES

1. INTRODUCTION

Rule (1) constrains the distribution of finite predicates in the sentence so drastically that it places on non-finite verb forms the entire burden of creating complex sentences. But despite the ingenuity with which they utilized, non-finite verbs provide no solution to a number of serious problems that crop up in the grammar of complex sentences. According to Rule (1) no finite predicate can appear in a subordinate or co-ordinate clause that precedes and is dependent on the root clause. Since predicate nominals lack non-finite counterparts, they cannot be embedded; so if a predicate happens to be lexically realized as a noun, it cannot occur in a dependent clause. Any verb form that encodes an illocutionary force, such as the imperative, also has this same skewed distribution: its occurrence is restricted to the root clause. Certain defective verbs, such as the Kannaḍa modal auxiliary *bēku* 'must', which lacks non-finite forms, are similarly constrained. Lexical and morphological restrictions such as these permit greater freedom of grammatical variation in root clauses than in dependent clauses.

These morphological and lexical restrictions lead us up against some syntactic obstacles. The constraint against the embedding of predicate nominals creates a disparity between root and dependent clauses: while any of the four kinds of simple sentence may appear in a root clause, only those two kinds with a verbal predicate can occur in a dependent clause. Another problem involves the formation of direct discourse. Example (12)b has already illustrated a case of indirect discourse. Since indirect discourse is more marked than direct discourse, the presence of the former in a language always implies the presence of the latter. Therefore example (12) b should also indicate the presence of direct discourse. However, Rule (1) prohibits the embedding of finite predicates, and therefore precludes the possibility of direct discourse altogether. It effectively frustrates any attempt to embed a finite predicate that appears in the reported speech under a root clause with a verb of reporting.

The solutions to these and similar problems crucially depend on two sets of devices that allow a finite predicate to appear in a dependent clause. The first set consists of verbs whose exceptional morphological properties permit them to function as complementizers of finite predicates. The second set includes certain clitics which behave like conjunctions. These two sets of devices provide solutions which turn out to be principled exceptions to

Rule (1). Therefore, as we introduce these exceptions to Rule (1), we will revise it to accommodate them.

2. TWO EXCEPTIONAL VERBS

This section is primarily concerned with two lexical exceptions to the constraint against multiple finite predicates in the Dravidian sentence. It introduces two verbs whose exceptional grammatical properties allow them to circumvent this constraint in a clever, surprising, yet principled way. These two verbs, whose reflexes are represented throughout the Dravidian family, are **ā-* 'become' (*DEDR* 333) and **en-* 'say, think' (*DEDR* 868). Following our analysis of these two verbs is a brief discussion of other predicates that can on occasion mimic their special grammatical behaviour.

The two verbs **ā-* 'become' and **en-* 'say, think' share a common property, one that is striking among the verbs of the Dravidian languages: they take as their direct objects expressions of any category and internal complexity without imposing on them any morphological marking of their objecthood. They take interjections, single words, phrases, complete sentences, or even whole chunks of discourse; they take nouns, verbs, or onomatopoeia with equal facility; they take finite and non-finite forms alike. They do not require their objects to undergo some morphological adjustment such as bearing a case-marker or assuming a non-finite verb form; and, in fact, they cannot do so. In Lakoff's (1970) terms, they are negative absolute exceptions to case-marking. Since the theory of case-marking is responsible for the morphological interpretation of direct objects, and not the theory of finiteness, the verbs **ā-* 'become' and **en-* 'say, think' shield their direct objects from the application and effects of Rule (1). And since these two verbs are negative absolute exceptions to case-marking, they need not subcategorize objects that are subject to case-marking, viz. nouns, but may take expressions of any category and form. This flexibility in subcategorization permits these two verbs to combine with an object that contains a formally finite predicate.

The secret to their success in overcoming the constraint against multiple finite predicates lies not just in their exceptional behavior with respect to case-marking, but also in the fact that they are verbs, and therefore enjoy all the formal and morphological privileges of that category. When they are inflected as non-finite verb forms, they can be embedded along with their objects in a larger syntactic structure according to the patterns discussed in Chapter I. Although inflected forms of these two verbs often function as complementizers and conjuctions, they belong morphologically and lexically to the class of verbs.[2] It is only on the hypothesis that they are verbs that we can appeal to their exceptionality regarding case-marking and their ability to have non-finite verb forms to explain how they can embed a finite predicate and thus overcome the constraint against multiple finite predicates in the Dravidian sentence. Even though case-marking cannot participate in the formation of complex sentences, as noted in Chapter I, verbs which are negative absolute exceptions to it can.

The following examples from six languages demonstrate the various uses to which reflexes of **en-* 'say, think' are put in the formation of complex sentences with multiple finite predicates.

(20) TAMIL

(a) *nāṉ avaṉ nallavaṉ e-ṉ-ṟu niṉai-kkir-ēṉ.*
I-nom he-nom good man-nom say-cp think-pres-1s
'I think that he is a good man.'

(b) *pāttirattai uṭai-tt-āy eṉ-ṟāl uṉṉai cummāka*
pot-acc break-pst-2s say-cond you-acc alone
viṭa-māṭṭēṉ.
leave-neg-fut-1s
'If you broke the pot, I won't leave you, alone.'

(c) *avaṉ iṅkē va-nt-āṉ en-patu uṇmai tāṉ.*
he-nom here come-pst-3sm say-vn-nom truth-nom indeed
'It is true that he came here.'

(d) *avaṉ cettuppō-ṉ-āṉ eṉ-kiṟ-a ceyti kēṭ-ṭ-ēṉ*
he-nom die-pst-3sm say-pres-adnp news hear-pst-1s
'I heard the news that he died.'

(21) KANNḌA

(a) *nannannu nanna pāḍige biṭṭu-biḍi en-d-aḷu jānaki.*
I-acc I-gen place-dat leave-imp say-pst-3sf Janaki
'Janaki said, "Leave me alone." '

(b) *emtīārinalli dōse tin-ōṇa anta mane*
MTR-loc dosai eat-hrt say-cp home
biṭ-ṭu hora-ṭ-a.
leave-cp start-pst-3sm
'He left the house to eat dosai at the MTR.'

(c) *śankara yāru gellu-t-āre ennu-vud-annu*
Sankara-nom who-com win-pres-3sh say-vn-acc
oppuvud-illa.
agree-npst-neg
'Who does Sankara not agree that (he) will win?'

(22) KONḌA

(a) *mā buba ṛey-n-a i-R-an.*
my father-nom beat-fut-1s say-pst-3sm
'My father said, "I will beat (you)." '

(b) *u-ṇ-a* *i-Riŋa* *anam* *siled.*
eat-fut-1s say-cond food-nom be-neg-fut-3sn
'There is no food for me to eat,' lit., 'There is no food if I say, "I will eat."'

(c) *ḍaŋ* *iz-i* *pīt-ta* *ṛis-t-an.*
ḍaŋ-onom say-cp fart-cp leave-pst-3sm
'He farted with a bang.'

(23) KŪVI

(a) *ēvasi* *nehasi* *inj-ihī* *nānu* *nam-i-ʔī.*
he-nom good man-nom say-cp I-nom believe-fut-1s
'I believe that he (is) a good man.'

(b) *ē* *samomita* *ro* *mosali* *ānataki*
that time-loc one crocodile-nom why
tirv-i *man-j-i* *inj-ihī* *buṛhaʔā̃* *vec-c-e.*
wander-cp be-pst-2s say-cp old man-acc ask-pst-3sn
'At that time a crocodile asked the old man, "Why are you wandering about?"'

(c) *nakka* *ōho* *mosali!* *nakka* *koḍḍaʔ ā̃* *ah-mu*
fox-gen 0 crocodile-voc fox-gen leg-acc arab-imp
inj-eliʔe *nakka* *koḍḍaʔā̃* *pissa-naha* *mosali* *tīmeri*
say-inf fox-gen leg-acc release-cp crocodile-nom Timeri-gen
veʔalaʔa *as-t-e.*
root-acc grab-pst-3sn
'When the fox said, "O crocodile, grab the foxes leg," the crocodile released his leg and grabbed the root of the Timeri tree.'

(24) KOLAMI

(a) *ān* *sā-t-un* *en-a* *ar-t-an.*
I-nom go-impf-1s say-cp cry-pst-1s
'I cried because (lit. saying) I was going away.'

(b) *amd* *anu* *vā* *en-a* *iṭ-t-an.*
he-nom I-dat come-imp say-cp tell-pst-3sm
'He told me to come.'

(25) OLLARI

(a) *raytul* *ṭre* *ṭre* *in-ji* *siṇḍup-eṭi* *sāy-d-ar.*
farmer-nom *tre* *tre*-nom sạy-cp call-cp be-fut-3sm
'The farmer would call "tre tre" to the sheep.'

(b) *eṇḍrika* *boŋga* *ke-n-ed* *in-ji* *adin* *pakkan*
crabs-nom holes-acc do-pst-3pn say-cp it-gen side

bokka *kē-d-aṇ.*
hole-acc do-npst-3sm
'Claiming crabs dug the holes (in his neighbor's tank bund), he will dig a hole in its side.'

Careful study of these examples reveals the many uses to which the verb **en-* 'say, think' is put. It embeds predicate nominals in (20)a and (23)a; ordinary finite verbs in (20)b, c, d, (21)c, (22) a, d, (23)b, (24)a, and (25) b; imperatives and hortatives in (21)a, b, (23)c, and (24)b; and onomatopoeia in (22)a and (25)a. This verb itself appears in the following forms: the conjunctive participle in (20) a, (21) b, (22)c, (23) a, b, (24) a, b, and; (25) a, b; the conditional in (20)b and (22) b; the verbal noun in (20)a and (21)c; the adnominal participle in (20) d; the infinitive in (23)c; and finite forms in (21)a and (22)a. The verb **en-* 'say, think' has a full lexical meaning in (21)a, (22)a, 23c, and (25)b, but seems to have no lexical meaning in the other examples, where it functions as an empty verb. The distinction between those instances of **en-* that have a full lexical meaning and those that do not, corresponds to the distinction between forms that are base-generated and those that are transformationally inserted. What these two use of **en-*'say, think' share in common, allowing us to treat them as one lexeme, is that they both are negative absolute exceptions to case-marking.[3]

Reflexes of **ā-* 'become' serve similar functions in the formation of complex sentences, as can be seen by studying the following sets of examples.

(26) TAMIL

(a) *avan̲* *va-nt-ān̲* *ān̲-āl* *nān̲* *avan̲ai*
he-nom come-pst-3sm become-cond I-nom he-acc
pārkka-villai.
see-pst-neg
'Though he came, I didn't see him.'

(b) *cāmān̲* *vāṅka* *ven̲ṭum* *ān̲-āl* *vāṅku*
goods buy-inf want-fut-3sn become-cond buy-imp
allatu *kaṭaiyai* *viṭ-ṭu* *iṛaṅku.*
become-neg-vn store-acc leave-cp get down-imp
'Unless you are going to buy something you want, leave the store.'

(27) KANNAḌA

(a) *yārū* *avana* *edurige* *āḍuttiralilla* *ādar-ū*
no one-nom he-obl with speak-pst perf-neg become-cond-and
heṅgasara *mūlaka* *ī* *mātu* *kāvēriya* *kivi*
women-obl through this word Kaveri-obl ear
muṭṭuttittu.
reach-pst perf-3sn

'Even though no one had spoken directly to him, word of this matter reached Kaveri's ear through women's gossip.'

(b)

veṅkamma	*tān*	*iru-v-a*	*sthaḷavannu*	*hēḷ-id-aḷu*
Venkamma-nom	self	be-fut-adnp	place-acc	fell-pst-3sf

allade	*tānu*	*ūru*	*biṭ-ṭu*	*allige*
become-neg-cp	self-nom	town	leave-cp	there-dat

hō-d-a	*saṅdarbhavannu*	*vivaris-id-aḷu.*
go-pst-adnp	circumstance-acc	detail-pst-3sf

'Venkamma not only told them her position, but also explained the circumstances under which she had left town.'

(28) PENGO

(a)

hī-d-n-ay	*ac-i*	*hī-d-a.*[4]
give-tp-fut-2s	become-cond	give-tp-imp

'If you are going to give (it) to me, give it.'

(b)

ē	*buḍiyaŋ*	*acek*	*dan-sampati*	*ā-t-at-e*
that	wife-dat	much	wealth-wealth-nom	become-pst-3sn-and

pa	*tā*	*manto*	*haluta*	*vari.*
even	self-gen	mind-loc	be-neg-pst-3sn	joy-nom

'Although that woman had so much wealth, she was not contented.'

(29) PARJI

(a)

in	*nāto*	*andar*	*paṭ-ṭ-o*
you-obl	what	confusion-nom	befall-pst-3sn

mĕ-d-a	*agi*	*īn*	*bulkak-mo-t.*[5]
be-fut-3sn	become-cp	you-nom	err-pres-2s

'What confusion has overcome you that you make such a mistake?'

(b)

met-t-ed	*er-oḍ*	*penda*	*katrano*	*āy*
be-pst-3sn	become-cond	forest field-nom	cut-vn-nom	be

'As conditions were proper, he said, "The forest field ought to be cleared."'

The verb **ā-* 'become' embeds predicate nominals in (28) b; ordinary finite verbs in (26)a, (27)a, b, (28)a, and (29)a, b; and imperatives and defective verbs in (26)b. It appears as a conditional in (26) a, b, (27)a, (28)a, and (29)b; as a verbal noun in (26)b; as a negative verbal participle in (27)b; as a conjunctive participle in (29)a; and as a finite verb in (28)b. The verb **ā-* 'become' has some suppletive variants: *er-* is the stem variant that appears in the Parji conditional, *al-* in the Tamil and Kannaḍa negative conjugations. Unlike **en-* 'say, think' which commonly appears in both finite and non-finite forms when it embeds a finite predicate, **ā-* 'become' most commonly appears in non-finite form. Even the finite form *ātat* 'it became' in (28)b functions like the non-finite concessive conditional form, because it is embedded by the clitic *-e* 'even' whose properties are discussed in the next section. Non-finite forms of **ā-* 'become' are susceptible to contraction (Steever 1987) : the Tulu "subjunctive" particle *-ḍe*, the Kolami conditional suffix *-te*, and the concessive conditional suffix *-tiri*, all of which combine with finite predicates, descend from **ā-ḍe*, **ā-te*, and **ā-tiri*, respectively. These reconstructed forms are all non-finite forms of **ā-* 'become'.

The motivation to insert inflected forms of **ā-* 'become' into these structures for the purpose of embedding finite predicates rests syntactically on the fact that **ā-* 'become', like **en-* 'say, think', is a negative absolute exception to case-marking, and cannot alter the morphology of its direct object. What motivates the choice between the insertion of **ā-* 'become' and **en* 'say, think', however, is not clear at this point. Preliminary study suggests that the insertion of **ā-* is favored when some comparison or contrast is made between the two clauses it joins. In (27) b, for example, the extent to which Venkamma reveals information about herself exceeds what is expected. In (28)b the wife's great wealth is contrasted with her discontent. In (29) b the present seasonal conditions favor the clearing of the forest more than at any other time. The verb **ā-* 'become' may be used to make such comparisons because it expresses a transition from one state to another, during which a single entity—perhaps the standard of comparison—continues unaltered. But this speculation deflects us from our primary course, and must be deferred to some future study of Dravidian complementation. What matters for our present purpose is the fact that both **ā-* 'become' and **en-* 'say, think' share in common the property that they are negative absolute exceptions to case-marking. Since they cannot morphologically alter the form of their direct objects, they may freely combine with finite predicates. And since these finite predicates are interpreted as the direct object of these verbs, they are exempt from the application of Rule (1).

More Exceptions to Case-Marking

Since both **ā-* 'become' and **en-* 'say, think' occur throughout the Dravidian family in their capacity to embed finite predicates, they may both be reconstructed to Proto-Dravidian in this special capacity. However, scrutiny of the grammars of individual daughter languages produces a long list of predicates that may on occasion mimic the ability of these two verbs to embed finite predicates, and so pass temporarily into the class of predicates that are negative absolute exceptions to case-marking. Since the list varies from one language to another, we cannot reconstruct specific lexemes to the proto-language in this capacity, but merely the general tendency of certain classes of predicates to behave this way. Most common among this list are predicates of perception, cognition, communication, and comparison. Examples include Tamil *colla* 'tell', *pārkka* 'look at', *teriya* 'be known', *pōla* 'resemble', *ceyti* 'news', *mātiri* 'likeness'; Old Tamil *cettu* 'perceive alike'; Toda *nwīṭ* 'look at'; Kannaḍa *hēḷu* 'tell', *kēḷu* 'listen', *nōḍu* 'look at', *gottu* 'knowledge', *nija* 'truth, fact'; Old Kannaḍa *gettu* 'perceive alike'; Telugu *ceppu* 'tell', *vinu* 'listen', *telusu* 'be known', *nijam* 'truth, fact'; Pengo *huṛ* 'see'; Konḍa *ven* 'hear', *veR* 'tell'; Parji *cūṛ* 'look at'. Note that both nouns and verbs are represented in this list : Tamil *ceyti* 'news', Kannaḍa *gottu* 'knowledge', and Telugu *nijam* 'truth, fact' are nouns.

The following examples illustrate how other predicates can embed a finite predicate in imitation of **ā-* 'become' and **en-* 'say, think'.

(30) TAMIL

(a) *nī* *eṉṉa* *ceñ-cu* *iru-kka-ṇum* *teriyum-ā* ?
you-nom what do-cp be-inf-must know-fut-3sn-int
'Do you know what you must do ?'

(b) *anta* *āḷu* *rompa* *nallavaṉ* *mātiri*
that man-nom very good man-nom likeness
iru-kk-aṉ *pār-tt-iy-ā* ?
be-pres-3sm see-pst-2s-int
'Did you see how good that that man is?'

(c) *intirā* *cuṭap* *paṭ-ṭ-ār* *ceyti*
Indira-nom shoot-inf befall-pst-3sh news-nom
vēkamāka *paravi* *...kiṭai-tt-atu.*
quickly spread-cp obtain-pst-3sn
'The news that Indira was shot spread and quickly reached us.'

(d) *...moy-tt-a* *tumpi* *paẓam*
swarm-pst-adnp bee-nom fruit-nom
cettu...(*naṟṟiṇai* 35.3)
think like-cp
'Thinking that the swarming bees were a fruit...'

(31) TODA

(a) *i* *mox* *ï.* *xïs-s-k* *nwī·ṭ-k-in.*
this boy-nom what do-pst-3s see-fut-ls
'I will see what this boy did.'

(b) *aθ* *inu* *nwī·ṭ-k-in.*
that-nom what-nom see-fut-ls
'I will see what that is.'

(32) KANNAḌA

(a) *niṅge* *eṣṭu* *uṣṇa* *āgide*
you-dat how heat-nom become-pres prf-3sn
gott-ā ?
knowledge-nom-int
'Do you know how hot it has become ?'

(b) *ēn̲u* *māḍa* *bēku* *hēḷu.*
what do-inf must tell-imp
'Tell me what I must do.'

(c) *nānu* *hēḷ-t-īni* *kēḷu.*
I-nom tell-press-ls listen-imp
'Listen to what I am telling you.'

(d) *pasarise* *tumbi-gaḷ* *kuvalayaṅgal* *aral-du-ve*
spreading bee-pl-nom water-lily-pl open-pres-3np
gettu ...(*pāmpa bharata* 5.63).
think like-cp
'Thinking that the clustered bees were a blossoming water-lily.'

(33) TELUGU

(a) *āyanuku* *kāsta* *dhairyam* *nīwu* *cepp-ali.*
he-dat little courage-nom you-nom say-perm
'You might say that he has little courage.'

(b) *cep-t-ānu* *vinu.*
say-fut-ls listen-imp
'Listen to what I am going to say.'

(34) KONḌA

(a) *embe* *so-R-a* *ma-n-an* *veR-si* *sī-d-a.*[6]
where go-pst-tpe be-fut-3sm tell-cp give-tp-imp
'Tell me where he has gone.'

(b) *nān* *unṟi* *māṭa* *veR-n-a* *ve-n-id* *a*?
I-nom one word tell-fut-1s listen-fut-2s int
'Will you listen to what I am going to tell you?'

(35) PARJI

(a) *nāto* *rōn* *paṭ-ṭ-o* *mĕ-d-a*
what-nom crying befall-pst-3sn be-fut-3sn
cūṛ-i *ver.*
see-cp come-imp
'See what (woman) is crying and come (back).'

These predicates exhibit a high degree of variation: they are nouns in (30)b (*mātiri* 'likeness'), c, and (32)a; elsewhere they are verbs. They may appear in dependent clauses, (30) b, c, d, (35)a, and (32)d, or in root clauses in the remaining examples. They embed a wide variety of finite predicates: imperatives and the like in (30)a and (32) b; predicate nominals in (30) b, d, (31)b, (32)d, and (33)a; and ordinary finite verbs elsewhere. Virtually all of these examples may have counterparts in which some form of **ā-* 'become' or **en-* 'say, think', such as the conjunctive participle, may appear between the matrix verb and the finite predicate it embeds. The examples without these additions often carry a connotation of rushing or hurry, of insistence or immediacy. It is sufficient for our purposes to note that such predicates temporarily migrate into the class of verbs that are negative absolute exceptions to case-marking, and that when they do, they behave like *ā- 'become' and *en- 'say, think'.

Our discussion of complex sentences has up to this point studiously avoided reference to the North Dravidian subgroup. But the examples we have just examined will help us better to understand the momentous changes that have taken place in the syntax of this subgroup. The use of non-finite verb forms is less prevalent, and the descriptive capacity of Rule (1) is accordingly diminished. One major reason for this change is that many verbs capable of taking a complement have in this subgroup passed irrevocably into the class of verbs that are negative absolute exceptions to case-marking. That is to say, many matrix verbs may directly combine with a complement clause containing a finite predicate without the intervention of any grammatical device to block the application of Rule (1). Inspection of the following Kurux examples confirms this.

(36) KUṚUX

(a) *ās* *adin* *pāṛ-age* *sikhabācas.*
he-nom she-acc sing-inf teach-pst-3sm
'He taught her how to sing.'

(b) *ās* *barʔon* *bācas*
he-non come-fut-ls say-pst-3sm
'He said he would come.'

(c) *en* *asra* *nan-d-an* *enghae* *sannias*
I-nom desire do-pres-ls I-gen friend-nom
bar ʔ os.
come-fut-3sm
'I hape that my friend will come.'

Example (36)a contains a matrix verb *sikhbācas* 'he taught' which governs the infinitive *pāṛage* 'to sing' in' a dependent clause. Such examples are not as common, however, as those in (36)b and c where matrix verbs directly embed finite predicates.

Many of the examples that have been analyzed as instances of parataxis in the literature may now be treated as constructions in which a negative absolute exception to case-marking embeds a finite predicate. These exceptions help us effectively to redress the various discrepancies noted above: they permit the formation of direct discourse and the embedding of predicate nominals in dependent clauses.

Revision of Rule (1)

A revision of Rule (1) is in order so that it will accurately predict the distribution of finite predicates in the Dravidian sentence, as exemplified in this section. Only one class of verbs, negative absolute exceptions to case-marking, induce the exceptional behaviour found in these examples, so their impact on Rule (1) may easily be localized. To state the revision in compact form, a certain amount of terminology is introduced. The position specially designated for finite predicates by Rule (1) occurs in the root clause of the sentence, a location that is called the ROOT DOMAIN OF FINITE PREDICATES, or RDFP for short. The revision is prompted by predicates which are exceptions to case-marking, and include the common Dravidian verbs **ā-* 'become' and **en-* 'say, think', as well as others in individual languages, e.g. Kannaḍa *hēḷu* 'say', Konḍa *veR* 'tell', Parji *cūṛ* 'see', Tamil *ceyti* 'news', Kannaḍa *gottu* 'knowledge'. Such a predicate is called a FINITE PREDICATE EMBEDDING PREDICATE, or FPEP. Each FPEP introduces a finite predicate in a dependent clause, and in doing so defines a DEPENDENT DOMAIN OF FINITE PREDICATES, or DDFP, in the sentence c-commanded by the FPEP. With these terms at our disposal let us now restate Rule (1).

(37) RULE FOR THE DISTRIBUTION OF FINITE PREDICATES

(a) The Dravidian sentence has exactly $n+1$ finite predicates, where n equals the number of FPEPs in the sentence, and *1* stands for the finite predicate in the root clause.

(b) The finite predicate in the RDFP occurs highest and rightmost in the constitutent structure; commands all other predicates in it; and is itself commanded by none. Each FPEP induces a DDFP. The finite predicate in each DDFP occurs highest and rightmost in the S that is commanded by the FPEP; commands all other predicates in the DDFP; and is itself commanded by none.

(c) All remaining predicates in the sentence are non-finite.

This rule correctly predicts the number and location of finite predicates in the Dravidian sentence in all other the examples examined so far.

3. SOME EXCEPTIONAL CLITICS

Not only do FPEPs combine with finite predicates to form complement clauses, but certain clitics do so as well. Certain clitics in the Dravidian languages may combine with finite predicates to embed them in dependent clauses. The capacity to do so stems in part from the fact that these clitics often instantiate quantifiers. Quantifiers share much in common with conjunctions : the two differ principally in that quantifiers ennumerate the members of a set by means of set description whereas conjunctions do so by means of definite description. This close tie between the two is brought into relief by a historical development in some Dravidian languages where

Indo-Aryan conjunctions and complementizers are borrowed into Dravidian in exactly the position where native FPEPs and clitics are found to occur. Since the borrowed forms are independent words and lack a Dravidian morphology, they tend to establish themselves as a new word-class into which inherited Dravidian clitics and FPEPs may be attracted by virtue of similar function.

The following examples illustrate the variety of complex sentences in which clitics embed finite predicates.

(38) TAMIL

(a) *avaṉ nāḷiakku varu-v-āṉ-ō eṉakku cantēkam.*
he-nom tomorrow come-fut-3sm-*or* I-dat doubt-nom
'I doubt whether he will come tomorrow.'

(b) *avaṉ kālaiyil cāppiṭ-ṭ-ān-ō cāppiṭa-villaiy-ō.*
he-nom morning-loc eat-pst-3sm-*or* eat-neg-pst-*or*
'I don't know whether he ate this morning or not.'

(c) *yār aṅkē mutalil vantu cēru-v-ār-ō*
who-nom there first come-cp reach-fut-3sh-*or*
avar ṭikeṭṭu vāṅkalām.
he-nom ticket buy-perm
'Let whoever reaches there first buy the tickets.'

(d) *nērru va-nt-āṉ-ē nāṉ avaṉai pār-tt-ān.*
yesterday come-pst-3sm-*even* I-nom he-acc see-pst-3sm
'I saw him, (you know) the man who came yesterday.'

(e) *eṉ koẓantaiy-ōṭa vāẓkkaiy-ē ippaṭi*
I-gen child-gen life-nom-emp thus
pāẓāyi-ṭ-um-nu eṉakku tōnalai-yē.
ruin-fut-3sn-*say-cp* I-dat appear-neg-3sn-emp
'I don't think that my child's life will be spoiled this way.'

(39) KANNAḌA

(a) *uḷida kālējugaḷalli prinsipālarige eṣṭu sambaḷa*
other college-pl-loc principal-pl-dat what salary
koḍu-tt-āre-yō aṣṭannu ivarige koḍuvante
give-pres-3p-*or* that-acc this man-dat give-as if
māḍis-id-aru.
'They had this man (i.e. me) paid as big a salary as the principals in other colleges were paid.'

(b) *ī sala yāke hīge āyit-ō gott(u) illa.*
this time why thus happen-pst-3sn-*or* knowledge-nom be-neg
'I don't know why this time it happened like this.'

(c) *monne* *bhaṣa* *ā-d-a* *mēle* *nimma*
d-b-y lecture-nom become-pst-adnp after you-obl
jōtēli *ba-nd-en-alla,* *āgalē* *hēḷa* *bēku*
with come-pst-1s-*tag* then talk-inf must-fut-3sn
antidde.
feel-pst-1s
'I felt I ought to talk to you then, (you know) after the lecture the day before yesterday.'

(40) TELUGU

(a) *ī* *ḍabbu* *ekkaḍa-nunci* *wacc-in-d-ō*
this money where-abl come-pst-3n-*or*
akkaḍa-kē *pampu.*
there-dat send-imp
'Send this money straight back to where it came from.'

(b) *āme* *ippuḍē* *rājyam-lō* *und-ō* *telīdu.*
she-nom now country-loc be-pres-3sn-*or* know-neg
'I don't know whether she is in the country now.'

(c) *snēhituḍa-wu-gadā* *kāsta* *wādiki* *naccajeppudū* ?
friend-nom-2s-*tag* little he-dat persuade-vn
'You are his friend, so couldn't you try to persuade him ?'

(41) KONḌA

(a) *embe* *nī* *iṣṭam* *ki-n-id-o* *bān* *iḍ ? a.*
where you-nom desire do-fut-2s-*or* there put-imp
'Put it wherever you want to.'

(b) *inṟo* *o-t-anṟ-e* *rinēṇḍe* *so-R-ad-o*
house-loc take-pst-3sm-*and* 2 day-nom go-pst-3n-*or*
munēṇḍe *so-R-ad-o.*
3 day-nom go-pst-3n-*or*
'It might be two or three days since he brought (him) home.'

(42) PENGO

(a) *karḍe* *gajakan* *ā-t-an-e*
boy-nom big one-nom become-pst-3sm-*and*
buḍiya *icat.*
wife-nom say-pst-3sf
'When her boy became big, the wife said . . .'

(b) *kosku* *ṭū-n-ar-ār-e* *lay* *vanj-n-ik* *ayak.*
fowl-pl kill-fut-3pm-*and-and* rice boil-fut-3pf woman-pl
'The men slaughter the fowls, and the women prepare the rice.'

(c) *punakader* *kēr-aṭ* *ar* *punvakader*
know-vn-3p sing-hort and know-neg-vn-3p
ici *ēnd-aṭ.*
say-cp dance-hort
'Let those who know, sing, and, as for those who do not, let them dance.'

(43) KOLAMI

(a) *attin* *sera-t-un-te* *amdun* *ōla-t-un.*
there go-fut-ls-*cond* he-acc see-fut-ls
'When/if I go there, I'll see him.'

(b) *epuḍ* *epuḍ* *van-n-en* *apuḍ* *apuḍ* *an* *tinekanni* *ol-n-en.*
when when com-pst-3sm then then my eat-vn-acc see-pst-3sm
'Whenever he came, he always saw me eating.'

(44) KUṚUX

(a) *ās* *ammu* *onn-d-as* *awr* *nīn*
he-nom water drink-pres-3sm and you-nom
ṭaṭxa *mox-d-ay*
mango eat-pres-2s
'He drinks water and you eat mango.'

(b) *eka* *ālas* *isan* *bar-c-as* *ās* *inna*
which man-nom here come-pst-3sm he-nom today
pairi *keras.*
morning go-pst-3sm
'The man who came here left this morning.'

(c) *ās* *eksan* *keras* *adin* *baldan.*
he-nom where-acc go-pst-3sm it-acc know-neg-pres-1s
'I do not know where he went.'

(d) *ād* *isan* *enderge* *bar-c-a* *ka* *ekase* *bar-c-a*
she-nom here why come-pst-3sf or how come-pst-3sf
adin *nēhũ* *balnar.*
it-acc no one-nom know-neg-pres-3p
'No one knows why she came here or how she came here.'

The clitic *-ō* 'or, whether' may embed a finite predicate in two kinds of constructions dubitative constructions and correlative relative clauses. The use of a quantifier with the basic meaning of disjunction is natural in a dubitative construction since doubt is a propositional attitude that expresses the inability to choose among several alternatives. In (37)b both alternatives are explicitly stated, and each of the alternative propositions contains a finite predicate embedded by an instance of *-ō* 'or'. Although there is only one disjunction semantically in (37)b, it is mechanically copied to each surface occurrence of a finite predicate by CONJUNCTION-SPREADING. Just as often, however, only one alternative is expressly stated, as in (37)a, (39)b. More interesting, perhaps, is the use of *-ō* 'or, whether' in the formation of correlative relative clauses, as in (37)a, (38)a, (39)a, and (40)a.[7] The lower clause of the correlative has a finite predicate that is embedded by *-ō* 'or'. The upper clause contains a proposition the truth of which is satisfied by a range of alternative conditions expressed by the propositional abstract in the lower clause. The abstract is a proposition with a gap formally marked by an interrogative pronoun which is correlated with a demonstrative pronoun in the upper clause, and which defines the range of alternatives to be explored in the satisfaction of the proposition. Here, as in the dubitative construction, the quantifier *-ō* 'or, whether' marks a set of alternatives.

A brief digression into the historicity of correlative relative clauses in the Dravidian languages is necessary to dispel some misconceptions about their source. With the notable exception of Lakshmi Bai (1985), most Dravidian linguists have thought that the correlative constructions were borrowed in Dravidian from Indo-Aryan. This notion rests on two fallacies, one material and the other methodological. First, correlative clauses are found throughout the Dravidian family with much the same structure: the principles of comparative reconstruction would dictate their presence in the proto-language. More compelling is the fact that Dravidian correlative clauses tend to use some kind of quantification to join together the two clauses of the correlative construction. Although use of the clitic *-ō* 'or, whether' is the most widespread, the use of pairs of reduplicated interrogative and demonstrative pronouns is also attested, as in (42)b. To the best of my knowledge, Indo-Aryan correlative clauses do not make much use of quantification to form correlative constructions. Second, the notion that correlative relative clauses come from Indo-Aryan rests on the fallacy that a language or a language family should have only one strategy for forming relative clauses, one which empirical evidence the world over refutes. So much attention has been devoted to the study of relative clauses created with the adnominal participle that the correlative strategy is considered alien. But this is an accident of the development of Dravidian linguistics, not the Dravidian languages. Once again, the distribution of correlative constructions throughout the family, coupled with the fact that these kinds of relative clauses and those formed with the adnominal participle have complementary functions (Ramasami 1981), invalidates this contention. Even if the hypothesis of borrowing were maintained, it would still beg the question of what structural properties of the Dravidian sentence would permit such a borrowing to take place. Correlative relative clauses may safely be said to be Dravidian in their grammar.

A second variety of correlative relative clause may be seen in (37)d where the clitic quantifier *-ē* 'even, and' embeds a propositional abstract with a finite predicate under the matrix clause. While *-ē* 'even, and' is semantically a quantifier, syntactically it is a cataphoric particle: it may be treated as an instruction to seek additional information about some preceding entity or action in what follows. This clitic is thus well-suited by its semantics and syntax to the formation of correlative clauses. In (37)a it appears to subordinate one clause to another, but in (40)b and (41)a it co-ordinates the components of the construction. In both cases, however, the content of one clause restricts the interpretation of the other. All instances of *-ē* 'even, and' share in common the ability to embed a finite predicate in a dependent clause.

Examples (38)c and (39)c exhibit a kind of parenthetical expression or non-restrictive relative clause that is rarely mentioned in the literature (Bright 1958: 48, Krishnamurti and Gwynn 1985: 285, and Sridhar 1987 are exceptions: the TAG-CORRELATIVE CLAUSE. In this construction a tag-question marker, derived from an inflected form of **ā-* 'become' and the interrogative morpheme *-ā*, simultaneously joins two clauses and embeds a finite predicate in a dependent clause. The function of these constructions, created with the aid of a tag-question marker, closely resembles the correlative clauses already examined; hence, the name Tag-Correlative Clause. The Kannaḍa form *-alla* in (38)c is derived from *alla* 'it does not become', an inflected form of **ā-* 'become', and the interrogative particle *-ā*, i.e. from *alla-*(*v*) *ā* 'isn't it?' Its status as a clitic is guaranteed by its phonological properties: only clitics such as *-ō* 'or' and *-ā* can prevent the deletion of the final *-n* in the finite verb form *banden* 'I came' in (38)c. The Telugu form *-gadā* (also *-kada*) is derived from *kādu* 'it does not become', an inflected form of **ā-* 'become', and the interrogative clitic *-ā*, i.e. from *kādā* 'isn't it so?' Although its status as a clitic is not as clear as that of its Kannaḍa cognate, the initial voicing of *k-* into *g-* and the loss of vowel length, both of which weaken its foothold in the paradigm of **ā-* 'become', suggest an evolution in this direction. Both forms can enter the set of clitics that embed finite predicates by virtue of the ability they inherit from **ā-* 'become' to embed finite predicates.

This line of development is carried one step further in (42)a where the conditional clitic *-te* in Kolami evolved from the conditional form of **-ā* 'become', viz. **ā-te* 'if becomes' through the cliticization of the inflected verb form and its subsequent contraction through the loss of the lexical root *ā-* 'become'. This change has also overtaken the concessive conditional clitic *-tiri* in Kolami and the so-called subjunctive clitic *-ḍe* in Tulu (Steever 1987). Cliticization and contraction are also evident in Tamil: the clitic *-nu* in (37)e is a contracted form of the conjunctive participle *eṉṟu* 'saying' (the conditional form *eṉṟāl* 'if says' is also contracted into *-nā*). Specialized forms of **ā-* 'become' and **en-* 'say, think' thus replenish the set of clitics that embed finite predicates.

Another way to enlarge the class of clitics is to borrow semantically similar words from Indo-Aryan languages, particularly where they are contiguous to Dravidian languages. The infiltration of an Indo-Aryan conjunction, *ɔr* 'and', is shown in (41) a, b, and c. In the first stage of borrowing, only the native Dravidian clitic *-e* 'and' is present to conjoin two clauses, both with finite predicates; In the second stage, the Indo-Aryan conjunction *ār* 'and' combines with the native *-e* 'and', appearing exactly where the native clitic appears by itself to embed a finite predicate; and in the final stage, the native clitic is dropped altogether. Native clitics may be displaced by borrowed words with great ease because, it seems to me, clitics are marked with respect to independent words: they presuppose the existence of the free forms to which by definition they are cliticized, while independent words do not necessarily imply the existence of clitics. The more marked forms are sloughed in historical development. We see in (43) a the extent to which Indo-Aryan conjunctions have replaced Dravidian clitics in Kuṛux: only the conjunction *awr* 'and' appears where, on the basis of comparative data, a clitic is expected. The Indo-Aryan correlative construction has also superceded the inherited Dravidian construction illustrated above, passing perhaps through the intermediate stage represented by the Kolami construction in (42)b. Note how the matrix-complement construction in (43) c has assimilated in its structure to the correlative construction in (43)b, the interrogative pronoun *eskan* 'where' in the complement is correlated with the demonstrative pronoun *adin* 'it' in the matrix. Since such constructions no longer crucially involve quantification, and since there is no lexical restriction of the verbs that can appear in such a construction, the descriptive adequacy of Rule (37) is largely null. To indicate choice among alternatives in (43)d, where on historical grounds the Dravidian quantifier *-ō* 'or, whether' is expected, the word *ka* 'or' is used instead: it probably comes from the Indo-Aryan word *ki* 'or' and, perhaps, the Dravidian interrogative particle *-ā*.[8]

As long as the number and kinds of devices that embed finite predicates remains relatively small, so that they may readily be listed, the descriptive adequacy of Rule (37) is not called into question. But as soon as a new class of conjunctions and complementizers emerges to eclipse the set of inherited clitics, and as soon as the influx of predicates into the set of FPEPs is great enough to render the grammatical properties of its members unexceptional, the devices that correlate finiteness and sentence structure are in danger of losing the crucial role they play in the distribution of finite predicates in the Dravidian sentence. In such circumstances, Rule (37) will be supplanted by something essentially different. However, since this development has reached an advanced stage only in the north subgroup, Rule (37) remains in effect in the other three.

We have not discussed all the issues involved in the analysis of those clitics that embed finite predicates in dependent clauses. No attempt has been made to analyze those constructions in which finite predicates are embedded by the combination of a clitic and another word, e.g. Tamil

-e+oziya 'aside from'. Only a tentative explanation can be offered here for the ability of these clitics to shield finite predicates from the effects of Rule (1). As a class, clitics make no morphological demands on the expressions with which they combine (unlike postpositions, say, which govern a particular case). In fact, they are so morphologically neutral that they generally fail to distinguish between noun and verb, and may readily combine with either category. (To be sure, idiocratic distinctions exist—Tamil *-um* 'and' does not combine with finite verbs.) Clitics are thus capable of preserving the morphological character of the expressions with which they combine and, in particular, do not alter the morphological markings of finite predicates. Their morphological neutrality allows them to combine with finite predicates, and so be accommodated in revised Rule (37), as described here below.

Further Revision of Rule (1)

Another term must be introduced here: any clitic that combines with a finite predicate so as to embed it in a dependent clause is called a FINITE PREDICATE EMBEDDING CLITIC, or FPEC. The set of FPECs includes, but is not exhausted by, **-ō* 'or, whether', **-ē* 'even, and', Kannaḍa *-alla*, Telugu *-gadā/-kadā*, Kolami *-te*, and spoken Tamil *-nu*. Each FPEC induces a DDFP, just as each FPEP does. A proviso must be made to the effect that there is one finite predicate for every *surface* manifestation of a FPEC to account for such sentences as (38)b and (40)b where the rule of Conjunction-Spreading has created multiple surface manifestations of a single quantifier in logical structure, each with a finite predicate. We may despite their obvious differences factor out what is common to both FPEPs and FPECs, and postulate a super-class of FINITE-PREDICATE EMBEDDERS or FPEs. The rule governing the distribution of finite predicates may now be restated.

(44) RULE FOR THE DISTRIBUTION OF FINITE PREDICATES

(a) The Dravidian sentence has exactly *n+1* finite predicates, where *n* equals the number of FPEs in the sentence (the number of FPECs being determined by the number of surface occurrences), and *1* stands for the finite predicate in the RDFP.

(b) The finite predicate in the RDFP occurs highest and rightmost in the constituent structure; commands all other predicates in it; and is itself commanded by none. Each FPE induces a DDFP. The finite predicate in each DDFP occurs highest and rightmost in the S that is commanded by the FPE; commands all other predicates in the DDFP ; and is itself commanded by none.

(c) All remaining predicates are non-finite.

This rule successfully predicts the distribution of finite predicates in all of the examples introduced up to this point, with the exception of the North Dravidian examples in this section.

A final word is in order concerning the markedness among the three principal sets of devices used to form complex sentences, viz. non-finite verb forms, FPEPs, and FPECs. Non-finite verb forms are the least marked. FPEPs are more marked because, even though they are often verbs with non-finite forms, their lexical entries must explicitly mention their exceptional behavior with respect to case-marking. FPECs are the most marked because, as clitics, they presuppose the existence of the independent words to which they are cliticized, while independent words make no comparable implication about the existence of clitics. Rule (44) incorporates these markedness relations to some extent. The non-finite verb forms are treated as relatively unmarked because they appear in the "elsewhere" clause of the rule. Since special mention must be made of FPEPs and FPECs, they are more marked than non-finite verb forms. FPECs are treated as the most marked because special provision must be made to determine the number of surface occurrences of a given FPEC.

4. SUMMARY

In introducing and analyzing two sets of principled exceptions to Rule (1), this chapter has dwelt at some length on the grammar of complementation in Dravidian. Further research in this area of grammar, in both the individual languages and the family as a whole, will pursue investigations of such diverse issues as constitutent structure, scope relations, lexical government, the semantic interpretation of individual constructions, and exhaustive cataloguing of FPEPs and FPECs. Though this chapter makes some modest contributions to the study of Dravidian complementation, it is primarily concerned to define the connection between finiteness and sentence structure in Rule (44). All this lays a proper foundation for the analysis of the serial verb construction in the remainder of the book. If, as we claim, the serial verb is truly characteristic of Dravidian grammar, it must be accommodated in a revision of Rule (44) with no disturbance of the rule's essential structure and content. If this can be done, it provides us with formal evidence that the serial verb constitutes part of the core grammar of Dravidian. The rest of this analysis attempts to validate our contention that the serial verb is well-integrated into the grammar of Dravidian.

Chapter Three

SERIAL VERBS IN SOUTH DRAVIDIAN

I. INTRODUCTION

HAVING considered the primary role that finiteness plays in Dravidian, we can now bring our attention directly to bear on the analysis of the SERIAL VERB FORMATION, or SVF. A provisional definition in Chapter I characterizes it as a construction that contains two or more finite verbs that mark agreement among themselves. When we apply the results of the two preceding chapters to this definition, we can formulate some working hypotheses about the nature of the SVF, its grammar, and its varieties. The next four chapters introduce pertinent evidence from the daughter languages to test them, and, ultimately, to vindicate the predictions they make about the place of the SVF in common Dravidian grammar. What we learn from this, the fourth and last set of exceptions to Rule (1), permits us to reconcile the SVF with the rules that govern the distribution of finite predicates in the Dravidian sentence.

Chapter II has already discussed how FPEs are used to generate constructions with multiple finite predicates. What criteria distinguish these FPE constructions from the SVF, which contains multiple finite verbs? Without distinctive criteria the FPE constructions would "capture" the SVF, assimilating it as a special case of a general phenomenon, and effectively do away with it as a separate construction. The two differ most clearly in their use of agreement: while the SVF requires agreement among its component parts, the FPE construction does not. After all, each FPE provides the opportunity to change the deictic center of the structure it appears in, and subject-predicate agreement features along with it. The single most important difference, however, derives from the distinction between predicates and verbs. In their respective definitions, the FPE construction refers to finite predicates, and the SVF to finite verbs. All remaining differences in their grammatical behavior may be directly attributed to this.

Each Dravidian sentence, Chapter I observes, consists of a subject and predicate; so, conversely, each predicate implies the prior existence of a sentence in which it is generated as a partial expansion. Therefore any expression such as a FPE that combines with a predicate necessarily combines with a sentence, as well. It follows that FPE constructions are complex sentence types such as matrix-complement structures. The proper domain of the FPE construction is therefore the sentence.

If the SVF is to be distinguished from FPE constructions, it must involve some fundamentally different constructions which have multiple finite verb forms. The logical place to look for the SVF, then, is the family of verbal constructions. Two obvious candidates present themselves: the compound verb construction (Steever 1983) and the co-ordinate verb construction. The evidence suggests that the prototypical SVF is a compound verb, while the remaining SVFs are co-ordinate verb constructions whose gross structural properties most closely approximate those of the compound verb construction. The proper domain of the SVF is therefore the set of verbal constructions.

The compound verb construction represents the prototypical SVF because it automatically satisfies the requirement that all the components of the SVF should have the same subject-verb agreement features. No matter how many component verb forms it has, the compound verb as a whole has just one logical subject, and hence one set of subject-verb agreement features (Steever 1983: 3, pass.). It follows that each SVF, no matter how internally complex, also has just one set of agreement features. These are encoded in the personal endings that appear on finite verb forms. The lack of contrast among the personal endings of the individual verbs in the SVF suggests that there is just one functionally finite verb in the structure, despite the multiplicity of forms. That one verb is the locus of all grammatical activity in the SVF: the personal endings of all the finite verb forms vary directly with those of the functionally finite verb. It owes this capacity to Rule (44): it occurs in the positions that are specially designated for finite predicates, and is therefore assigned agreement features by the very same process that so inflects any verb embeded by a FPE. Co-ordinate verb constructions can be SVFs to the extent they reproduce the superficial properties of compound verbs, e.g., they should obey a same-subject constraint that gives them the appearance of having one logical subject.

A transformational rule is proposed which expresses the relationship of direct variation among the personal endings of the SVF's component verbs. The rule that generates the SVF is a copy-rule: it replicates the personal ending (PE) of the head of the construction onto all of the remaining verbs within it, preserving the agreement features (AGR).

(45) A RULE TO GENERATE SERIAL VERB FORMATIONS

(a) Structural Description:

$$_V\Big[\underbrace{\Big[\text{VB}-\text{X}\Big]_1^n}_{1} + \underbrace{\begin{bmatrix}[\text{VB}-\text{Y}]-\text{PE}\\ \qquad [\alpha\text{AGR}]\end{bmatrix}}_{2}\Big]_V$$

(b) Structural Change:

$$_V\Big[\underbrace{\begin{bmatrix}[\text{VB}-\text{X}]\ -\text{PE}\\ \qquad [\alpha\text{AGR}]\end{bmatrix}_1^n}_{1} + \underbrace{\begin{bmatrix}[\text{VB}-\text{Y}]-\text{PE}\\ \qquad [\alpha\text{AGR}]\end{bmatrix}}_{2}\Big]_V$$

(c) Condition: Term 2, the head of the construction, must occupy a specially designated position for finite predicates.

Rule (45) is necessarily schematic so that it can cover many constructions and languages. It has to embrace compound verbs and co-ordinate verb constructions alike. Depending on the needs of the individual language and construction, further conditions may be required for the application of the rule. It might apply optionally or obligatorily; the (non-essential) variables *X* and *Y* might be further specified (including the possibility that *X* is null); extraneous material might separate terms 1 and 2; and so forth. What matters most for our present purpose is that Rule (45) captures the generalization that the personal endings of the SVF are non-contrastive, and vary directly with those on the head of the construction.

Rule (45) predicts that other grammatical phenomena may bear directly on the analysis of the SVF. It suggests the possibility of an alternation between a plain compound verb and a SVF, representing the input and output of Rule (45), respectively. This is in fact confirmed by three kinds of evidence : synchronic alternations in one language; historical alternations between two stages of a single language; and comparative alternations between two related languages. For example, the negative conjugation in Classical Tamil (pp. 42-44) and the *gi*-echo compounds in Kolami (p. 90) both provide synchronic evidence of this alternation. Thus, these languages independently generate constructions with the same properties as Rule (45)'s structural description. The existence of other agreement rules, independent of the structural change in Rule (45), further strengthens the postulation of that rule. Indeed, for reasons that are not clear to me,[1] the SVF thrives in languages where predicate nominals are inflected for subject-predicate agreement. What primarily concerns us here is that the structural description and change of Rule (45) exploit independently available forms and processes in the language.

Given the complementary relation of FPE constructions and the SVF, each application of Rule (45) occurs within a single RDFP or DDFP. No SVF in our corpus ever straddles the boundary marked by a FPE. FPE constructions mark agreement at the level of the sentence; the SVF, below the level of the sentence in a number of verbal constructions. Thus, these two kinds of constructions are accommodated at different levels of constituent structure.

Since the prototypical SVF is a compound verb, we will discuss what grammatical properties the SVF inherits from the compound verb. And since the other SVFs mimic the properties of these prototypical SVFs, we will discuss their grammar later.

The SVF may be classified in the same way that plain compound verbs are. Chapter I observes that compound verbs are primarily divided into auxiliary and lexical compound verbs, a distinction which clearly holds in the set of FPEs. Each of these divisions has its own characteristics: while the identity of the variables *X* and *Y* in Rule (45) may vary in auxiliary compound verbs, in lexical compound verbs it does not. This distinction is correlated with the basic difference between their respective functions: the auxiliary compound verb crucially utilizes the inflectional morphemes represented by *X* and *Y*, whereas the lexical compound verb exploits the two verb bases VB_1 and VB_2. The two most common auxiliary SVFs in Dravidian are the negative conjugation with the auxiliary **ā-* 'become', or one of its suppletive variants, and the perfect tense series with the auxiliary **man* 'be' (*DEDR* 4778). Although lexical SVFs tend to exhibit a broad range of varieties, three kinds appear over and over again in our samples: iterative compounds, balance compounds, and echo compounds. An iterative compound simply reduplicates the finite verb to convey intensity or repetition of an action. A balance compound (Mahapatra 1979: 191) designates a general activity by juxtaposing two finite verbs that represent special instances of the activity, e.g. 'celebrate' is represented by the collocation of 'sing' and 'dance'. An echo compound is a variety of iterative compound in which a phonologically altered copy of a finite verb is adjoined to the original. Its semantics are discussed in detail below.

Not all finite predicates are finite verbs; conversely, not all finite verbs are finite predicates. This stems from the fact that agreement in Dravidian may serve two different purposes, each in response to a different concept of finiteness. It may apply at the level of the sentence to mark agreement between a subject and its predicate, incidentally marking the extreme right boundary of the RDFP or DDFP in the sentence occurs. It may also apply below the level of the sentence to mark agreement among the components of a verbal construction, the SVF. In doing so it morphologically delineates the boundaries of that construction. In the first case we will speak of FUNCTIONAL FINITENESS, derived from the syntactic relation between a subject and its predicate; in the second FORMAL FINITENESS, derived from the relation between a verbal construction and its head. Although the second kind largely depends on the first, its presence in a language sets up a tension with the first kind. In a language with SVFs a formally finite verb does not always coincide with a functionally finite predicate, and redundantly mark the positions that Rule (44) designates for finite predicates. The loss of SVFs in some of the daughter languages seems partly a response to the conflict between the functional and formal concepts of finiteness (see Chapter Seven). The loss of SVFs means that the two concepts coincide: any verb that is formally marked as finite necessarily appears in the specially designated positions for finite predicates, and nowhere else.

The historical development of the SVF shows us just how independent of the FPE constructions it is. They evolve independently: while FPE constructions change in North Dravidian, some SVFs remain constant; conversely, while FPE constructions remain constant in South Dravidian, many SVFs change.

If FPE constructions and the SVF are based on different concepts of finiteness, and undergo different historical changes, how can they both be reconciled in a single revision of Rule (44)? It is reformulated to accommodate the SVF first by replacing the term finite predicate everywhere with the more precise term functionally finite predicate. Two clauses are then added to the rule to account for the SVF (see Rule (103) below). The grammar of each language must be specified as having certain rules such as Rule (45) or not, according as it has SVFs, or not. Any language with the resources to generate the SVF has a tension between the functional and formal concepts of finiteness, represented in (44)and (45), respectively. The loss of rules that generate the SVF resolves this tension in favor of functional finitness.[2] The relative markedness of the two is inscribed in Rule(103), affirming the priority of functional (unmarked) over formal (marked) finitenss in both synchronic and diachronic realms.

These preliminary remarks furnish us with sufficient terms and concepts to explore the catalogue of SVFs and to analyze them in the individual languages. We accordingly begin with the south subgroup and proceed through the remaining subgroups in the next three chapters.

2. TAMIL

The language of Classical Tamil, as recorded in the *Caṅkam* texts and early *bhakti* literature, contains numerous examples of SVFs, virtually all of which were lost sometime during the medieval period. Consider the following examples of the negative conjugation with the auxiliary verb *al-* 'not become' (*DEDR* 234), the suppletive variant of *ā-* 'become' in the negative.

(46) OLD TAMIL

(a) *cel-v-ēm all-ēm* (*puṟanāṉūṟu* 31.11).
go-fut-lp become-neg-lp
'We will not go.'

(b) *ceṉ-ṟ-ēṉ all-ēṉ* (*appar tēvāram* 2563.1).
go-pst-1s become-neg-1s
'I did not go.'

(c) *maruṇ-ṭaṉ-eṉ all-ēṉ* (*patiṟṟuppattu* 74.23).
be scared-pres prf-1s become-neg-1s
'I am not scared.'

(d) *uy-ntaṉ-ar all-ar* (*puṟanāṉūṟu* 100.9).
escape-pres prf-3p become-neg-3p
'They have not escaped.'

(e) *cey-k-u al-ēṉ* (*kāmpa rāmāyaṇam* 4.229.4).
do-fut-1s become-neg-1s
'I will not do it.'

(47) (a) *aṟi-(y)ēm* *all-ēm,* *aṟi-ntaṉ-am* (*aiṅkuṟunūṟu* 240.1).
know-neg-1p become-neg-1p know-pres prf-1p
'It is not that we do not know: we do know.'

(b) *kāṇ-ēm* *all-ēm,* *kaṇ-ṭaṉ-em* (*kalittokai* 9.9).
see-neg-1p become-neg-1p see-pres prf-1p
'It is not that we do not see: we have seen.'

(c) *kēḷ-ēm* *all-ēm,* *kēṭ-ṭaṉ-am* (*kāmpa rāmāyaṇam* 244.3).
hear-neg-1p become-neg-1p hear-pres prf-1p
'It is not that we do not hear: we have heard.'

The morphemic structure of all the examples in (46) is the same, despite some allomorphic variation among the repeated personal endings. The main verb consists of a verb base, a tense marker, and a personal ending; the auxiliary verb consists of the verb base *al-* 'not become', the negative morpheme, and a personal ending congruent with the main verb's. Both verb forms are finite, and can independently appear in the position specially designated for finite predicates. Example (46)e consists of the main verb *ceyku* 'I will do, make' and the auxiliary *aleṉ* 'I do not become': both -(*k*)*u* and *-eṉ* are allomorphs of the first person singular personal ending. The examples in (47) are rarer than those in (46), and tend to be formulaic. They contain a double-negative SVF which has the force of an emphatic affirmative. The double negative *aṟiyēm allēm* in (47)a consists of two finite verb forms, *aṟiyēm* 'we do not know' and *allēm* 'we do not become', each of which consists of a verb base, the negative morpheme, and a personal ending, and can appear independently of the other in the position specially designated for finite predicates. Negative SVFs similar to those in (46) are found throughout our survey.

A brief digression is in order here. It might be protested against our analysis that these examples need no special treatment because the auxiliary *al-* 'not become', a variant of *ā-* 'become', is independently a FPEP. The two cases differ syntactically: the FPEP combines with an entire sentence, but the auxiliary combines with a main verb to form a compound verb. There can be little doubt, however, that the exceptionality of *ā-* 'become' and *al* 'not become' with respect to case-marking ideally suits them to use in a SVF. Indeed, this property may help us to explain why in Muria Goṇḍi the negative conjugation has persisted and even grown while other SVFs have fallen by the wayside.

Interestingly enough, Classical Tamil furnishes us with a variant of the SVF that conveys negation. The forms in this paradigm are not SVFs, but plain compound verbs. Here the auxiliary *al* 'not become' combines with a non-finite form of the main verb, the bare verb base (bvb).

(48) (a) *maṟa-(v)al-ēṉ.* (*puṟanāṉūṟu* 395.32)
forget-bvb-become-neg-1s
'I will not forget.'

(b) *koḷḷ-al-ir.* (*ibid* 109.3)
receive-bvb-become-neg-2p
'You will not receive.'

(c) *cell-al-am.* (*ibid* 101.1)
go-bvb-become-neg-1p
'We do not go.'

(d) *vāẓ-al-aḷ.* (*akanāṉūṟu* 12.14)
live-bvb-become-neg-3sf
'She will not live.'

The similarity between the negative compound verbs in (46) and (48) is irresistable: it suggests the possibility of a structural alternation between the two. They appear to differ only in the use they make of Rule (45), which seems to apply in the derivation of (46) but not (48). Not enough is yet known about these examples to claim that the alternation is one of free variation and, hence, that Rule (45) applies optionally in the derivation of the negative paradigm with *al-* 'not become'. However, the kinship between the two is readily apparent.

It was suggested above that the presence of an agreement rule to create the congruent personal endings in a SVF usually implies the existence elsewhere in the grammar of an agreement rule that inflects predicate nominals for agreement with their subjects. Such a rule does exist in Classical Tamil, both in the positive and negative.

(49) (a) *nīr* *caṉṟ-īr.* (*puṟanāṉūṟu* 195.1)
you-h-nom noble man-nom-2h
'You (are a) noble man.'

(b) *avaṉ* *pukaẓ-aṉ.* (*ibid* 221.1)
he-nom fame-nom-3sm
'He is a man of fame.'

(c) (*nām*) *peṇṭ-ir-ēm* *all-ēm.* (*ibid* 246.10)
we-nom woman-p-1p become-neg-1p
'We are not women.'

The predicate nominals in (49) agree with their subjects in person, number, and, where appropriate, gender. Note particularly in (49)c that both the predicate nominal *peṇṭirēm* 'we women' and the negative verb *allēm* 'we do not become' are both inflected for congruent personal endings. We cannot yet assimilate this example to the negative SVFs in (46) because it is a noun-verb collocation, not a compound verb. More data and, perhaps, a more abstract analysis may eventually permit this identification, but for now the parallels are simply noted.

The classical texts offer us still more varieties of SVFs: some are compound verbs, others co-ordinate structures in which all the verbs have the same subject. In either case, the head verb is often a verb of simple motion or location.

(50) (a) *kaṉ-ṭaṉ-eṉ* *varu-v-al.* (*puṟanāṉūṟu* 23.17)
see-pres prf-1s come-fut-1s
'I will see and come.'

(b) *taṅk-iṉ-ir* *ceṉ-mō.* (*ibid* 233.7)
stay-pst-2p go-imp-(2p)
'Stay, (then) go.'

(c) *teri-ntaṉ-ar* *koḷ-am-ē.* (*tolkāppiyam col.* 295)
know-pres prf-3p hold-opt-(3p)-emp
May they understand (it).'

(d) *cēr-ntaṉ-ir* *cel-ku-vir.* (*akanāṉūṟu* 200.12)
join-pres prf-2p go-fut-2p
'They will reach/arrive there.'

(e) *irak-k-u* *vār-eṉ.* (*patiṟṟuppattu* 61.11)
beg-fut-1s come-neg-1s
'I do not come to beg.'

Although the syntactic analysis of these phrases varies from one example to the next, all are unquestionably SVFs. Example (50)c corresponds to the modern lexical compound verb *terintu koḷḷa* 'understand', example (50)d to the modern compound verb *cērntu pōka* 'arrive, reach'. The other SVFs in (50) are co-ordinate constructions whose component verbs all have the same subject, and correspond to co-ordinate structures in the modern language that use the conjunctive participle, not repeated finite verb forms. Whether a particular SVF is a compound verb or a co-ordinate structure is not always clear, but it is certain that the SVF as a class includes both kinds of structures.

It follows from what we have said that a SVF occurs whenever a finite verb form occurs anywhere other than the specially designated position stipulated for finite predicates in Rule (44). The following sentences contain examples which meet this characterization of the SVF in an interesting way: though they have finite verb forms outside of the specially designated position, they have non-finite verb forms inside of it.

(51) (a) *āṭ-iṉ-ir* *pāṭ-iṉ-ir* *cel-iṉ-ē.* (*puṟanāṉūṟu* 198.10)
dance-pst-2p sing-pst-2p go-cond-emp
'If you go celebrating (lit. singing and dancing)...'

(b) *ētt-iṉ-ar* *tar-ūum* *kūẓe.* (*ibid* 122.6)
praise-pst-3p give-fut-adnp wealth
'The wealth they bring in tribute/praise ...'

(c) *maṟa-ntaṉ-am* *tuṟa-nt-a* *kāẓ.* (*naṟṟiṇai* 172.2)
forget-pst-1p leave-pst-adnp seed
'The seed which we did forget ...'

(d) *vāẓtt-in̲-ar* *var-ūum* *iravalar*. (*puṟanāṉūṟu* 122.7)
praise-pst-3p come-fut-adnp beggar-p
'Beggars who come praising you/who continually praise you.'

The personal endings of the finite verbs in (51) vary with the understood agreement features of the non-finite verb that stands in a position which would have contained a finite predicate according to Rule (44) if some other morphological requirement had not pre-empted it. The context of (51) a, for example, requires the verb *cella* 'go' to be finite so it can replicate its personal endings on the balance compound *āṭiṉir pāṭiṉir* 'they celebrated', but since it stands in the protasis of a conditional sentence, it should appear in the non-finite conditional form. In all of these cases, the morphology imposed by the matrix clause on the complement predicate supercedes the requirements of Rule (44). Any one of these non-finite verb forms could be replaced by a syntactically equivalent finite verb form and a non-finite form of a FPEP such as *eṉa* 'say, think', e.g., *celiṉē* 'if goes' may be replaced by *ceṉṟir eṉiṉ* 'if X says that you went'; *tuṟanta* 'which left' by *tuṟantaṉam eṉṟa* 'which X says that we left'. Despite the syntactic and semantic equivalence of the two expressions, this style of poetry always favors the terser, non-analytic form. These examples still conform to the alternative characterization of the SVF as a construction which permits a finite verb form in any position other than the one specially designated by Rule (44).

The SVFs in (50) and (51) also have non-SVF counterparts that correspond to compound verbs in which non-finite forms such as the bare verb base (bvb), the infinitive (inf), or conjunctive participle (cp) appear outside of the specially designated position and combine with the verb inside it. Consider the following set of examples.

(52)(a) *nemiṭ-i* *koṇ-ṭu*. (*naṟṟiṇai* 22.4)
scoop-cp hold-cp
'As (X) was scooping it up.'

(b) *urai-kka* *va-nt-atu*. (*puṟanāṉūṟu* 28.7)
declare-inf come-pst-vn
'(X) came to declare.'

(c) *pō-tara*. (*kalittokai* 56.31)
go-bvb-give-inf
'to bring'

(d) *peyar-tara*. (*puṟanāṉūṟu* 259.1)
turn-bvb-give-inf
'to return'

(e) *acai-vara*. (*naṟṟiṇai* 20.4)
move-bvb-come-inf
'to move (towards)'

(f) *tuyal-vara.* (*akanāṉūṟu* 13.20)
swing-bvb-come-inf
'to oscillate'

Inspection and comparison of the examples suggests a loose correspondance between SVFs and plain compound verbs. Examples (50)a and c both resemble (52)b in their use of *vara* 'come' to convey the meaning of an action directed towards some goal as expressed by the first verb in the compound. Example (50)c resembles (52)a, not just in its use of the verb *koḷḷa* 'hold', but also in the fact that the SVF in (50)c gave way historically to the plain compound verb in (52)a. Example (51)b resembles (52)c and d; and example (51)d resembles (52)e and f. Here the pattern of variation is the one that we have already seen between the two varieties of the negative conjugation in (46) and (48). The conditions under which the plain compound verb employs a bare verb base, infinitive, or some other non-finite form have not yet been determined, and may well be lexically determined by the second verb in the compound.

The Loss of the SVF in Tamil and Malayāḷam

The use of the SVF in Classical Tamil steadily declined during the medieval period so that it had virtually fallen from the language by the dawn of the early modern period. The loss consisted in the elimination of Rule (45) from the grammar of Tamil, and was partly motivated by the need to overcome the tension between the functional and formal treatments of finiteness. By the early modern period a formally finite verb could appear only in the position reserved for finite predicates by Rule (44). Malayāḷam, which branched off from Tamil during the early medieval period, seems to have chosen a more radical way of eliminating the tension between the two treatments of finiteness. It lost its subject-verb agreement rules altogether, with the result that the sole criterion for the finiteness of a verb in the modern language is whether it appears in the position specially designated for finite predicates. There is no longer any redundant morphological marking to help us to identify the finite verb. Since Malayāḷam has no morphological interpretation of finiteness, there can be no tension between the two treatments of finiteness. Thus, the loss of the SVF in Tamil and of subject-verb agreement in Malayāḷam seems to be two expressions of the same historical process, differing only in degree. Both restrict the distribution of personal endings, but where Tamil permits them in the position for finite predicates, Malayāḷam disallows them everywhere. What precipitated the loss of the SVF in Tamil and what extended the ban on SVFs to all personal endings in Malayāḷam can be explained only after the intensive study of texts from the appropriate period. The need for a proximate cause is clear: since many languages retain SVFs, the tension between the two treatments of finiteness does not invariably precipitate changes to bring about the elimination of the SVF. There is no doubt that the simultaneous loss of subject-predicate nominal agreement rules contributed to the downfall of the SVF.

Echo SVFs in Modern Tamil

Although virtually all SVFs passed out of Tamil by the end of the medieval period, one construction can be found in the modern language which technically conforms to our definition of the SVF. This construction is generated by a compounding rule known as KI-ECHO FORMATION. It applies to verbs and nouns alike to create a distributive compound, which conventionally carries a pejorative connotation. Consider the following examples.

(53)(a) *māṭu* *varum.*
ox-nom come-fut-3sn
'Some oxen will come.'

(b) *māṭu-kīṭu* *varum.*
ox-*ki* echo-nom come-fut-3sn
'Some oxen or stuff like it will come.'

When *ki*-Echo Formation applies to the noun *māṭu* 'ox' in (53)a, it creates the echo compound noun *māṭu-kīṭu* 'oxen and the like' in (53)b. In the resulting compound the echo word *kīṭu* partially reduplicates the form of the echoed word *māṭu* 'ox'. The first syllable of the echoed word is replaced in the echo word by the standard syllable *ki*, which is short or long depending as the initial syllable of the echoed word is short or long. Words that begin in *ki* -or *kī* -do not themselves undergo this compounding rule, e.g. *kiḷi* 'parrot' cannot serve as the basis of the echo compound **kiḷi-kiḷi* 'parrots and the like' (which is virtually indistinguishable from a true distributive compound). If any echo compound is to be formed on such words, the echo word should begin with *hi* -or *hī*-, so that we obtain *kiḷi-hiḷi* 'parrots and the like'. But since *h*- belongs to the phonological periphery of Tamil, many speakers prefer to forgo making such a compound than to pronounce an initial *h*-.

The *ki*-echo compound occurs in "affective" grammatical contexts, e.g. negatives, modals, conditionals, future tense. As with other distributive compounds, the *ki*-echo compound expresses an indefinite quantification so that *māṭu-kīṭu* might be more precisely interpreted as "some things, of which cattle might be taken as an instance." Depending on the context, such a compound can be understood as referring to domestic animals in general, traffic hazards, the components of a dowry, and so forth. Above and beyond indefinite quantification, the *ki*-echo compound conventionally expresses strong pejorative overtones to the effect that the speaker neither likes nor cares about the matter at hand to specify the entity or action-referred to by the echo compound. Its use is a mark of racy language, and conveys much the same flavor as do *shm*-echo compounds in Yiddish-English, e.g. *fancy-shmancy, Oedipus-Shmoedipus, at least he loves his mother* !

ki-Echo Formation applies equally to verbs. When it does, it creates an echo word that has the same inflections as the echoed word on which it is based. In the case of nouns, on the other hand, only the echoed word has grammatical inflections. This difference might be attributed to the fact that nouns typically have simple combining forms, often identical with the root; whereas in Modern Tamil the verb root is not a free form, but must occur with inflections, *ki*-Echo Formation applies to both finite and non-finite verbs, but for our present needs we illustrate only its application to finite forms.

(54)(a) *pāttirattai* *uṭai-tt-āy* *eṉṟ-āl* *tōlai* *uri-pp-ēṉ.*
pots-acc break-pst-2s say-cond skin-acc peel-fut-1s
'If you broke the pots, I'll skin you alive!'

(b) *pāttirattai* *uṭai-tt-āy* *kiṭai-tt-āy* *eṉṟ-āl*
pots-acc break-pst-2s *ki*-pst-2s say-cond
tōlai *uri-pp-ēṉ.*
skin-acc peel-fut-1s
'If you broke the pots or did any such stupid thing, I'll skin you alive.'

(c) *avaṉ-ukkup* *paci-kkiṟ-atu*
he-dat hunger-pres-3sn
'He is hungry.'

(d) *avāṉ-ukkup* *paci-kkiṟ-atu* *kici-kkiṟ-atu.*
he-dat hunger-pres-3sn *ki*-pres-3sn
'He is always hungry, or some damn thing!'

The finite verbs *uṭaittāy* 'you broke' in (54)a and *pacikkiṟatu* in (54)c lay the foundation for the *ki*-echo compounds *uṭāittāy kiṭaittāy* 'you broke or did some such stupid thing' in (54)b and *pacikkiṟatu kicikkiṟatu* '(he) is always hungry, or some damn thing' in (54) d, respectively. These echo compounds conform to our definition of the SVF since all of their component parts are formally finite verbs marking tense and subject-verb agreement.

The *ki*-echo compound originates not in Modern Tamil, but in the Proto-Dravidian era. In a series of important papers Emeneau (1938a, 1938b, 1939) recorded its presence throughout the south, south-central, and central subgroups of the family. It rarely occurs in the classical literatures because of its colloquial, devil-may-care shadings,[3] but it can be reconstructed to the proto-language in view of its wide distribution.

How has the *ki*-echo compound survived into Modern Tamil when all other SVFs have disappeared? The grammatical process that generates *ki*-echo compounds is both simple and general—simple in that it creates compounds by means of a mechanical, uncomplicated echoing rule, and general because it applies to nouns and verbs alike. The rule Chomsky-adjoins the echo-word to the right of the echoed word, if the conditions for its application are met. Its structural description need not specify the lexical category of its operand, and allows a wide degree of latitude as to where it may occur in the syntactic structure. In these respects it differs from Rule (45). This further implies that the grammatical mechanism that makes the SVF possible is a general output condition of the kind mentioned in Rule (44), not simply a transformational rule such as (45). Consequently, the loss of Rule (45) in the medieval period did not bring about the loss of SVFs generated by means of *ki*-Echo Formation. Even though it does not result from the application of Rule (45), the *ki*-echo compound verb based on a finite form satisfies our definition of the SVF.[4]

The SVF in Traditional Tamil Grammar

It is fitting to note here that traditional Tamil grammar recognizes the presence of SVFs in Classical Tamil and provides for their analysis. This school of grammarians grew up independently of the Sanskrit grammarians: it two outstanding texts are *tolkāppiyam* (c. 100 BC) and *naṉṉūl* (c. AD 1000). Our discussion of the treatment of SVFs is confined to its presentation in *tolkāppiyam* and its commentatorial tradition, particularly *cēṉāvaraiyar's* commentary on the second book, *collatikāram* 'morphology'.

Whereas many of our modern grammars purport to generate well-formed sentences, the traditional grammars of India set out to generate well-formed words. The majority of grammatical statements about linguistic forms and processes are in this tradition formulated in terms of words and classes of words, not in terms of constituent structure or syntactic categories. Thus, any rule that describes the syntactic relations among various linguistic expressions will more likely than not make reference to words.

In this grammatical tradition the SVF is identified in part by the term *muṟṟeccam* which means 'finite verb (*muṟṟu*) that functions as a non-finite verb (*eccam*)'. In effect this term designates not the entire SVF but only those finite verb forms that do not occur in the position specially designated for finite predicates. In doing so it draws attention only to the marked use of finite verb forms as a means of marking agreement among the members of a SVF, and assumes that the unmarked use of finite verbs is to aid the identification of a finite predicate. The term *muṟṟeccam* is thus not an isolated label, but a grammatical concept embedded in many others.

In traditional Tamil grammar verbs, *viṉai*, are divided into two basic classes. The first one is called *muṟṟuviṉai* 'finite verb', and is morphologically defined as that set of words which consists of a verb base, tense marker, and personal ending. This term is a compound of the basic terms *muṟṟu* 'mature, complete, ripe' and *viṉai* 'verb': it designates a verb which is formally complete in that it marks as many inflectional categories as any single verb can, and syntactically complete in that is stands in the position designated for finite predicates, thereby closing or "completing" the sentence. The second class is called *eccam* 'non-finite verb', or 'deficient form, combining form'. It characterizes a set of verb forms that are morphologically complete and free, but which are syntactically "deficient" in that they must combine with some following word. In essence this term describes the combinatoric property of this word-class: all the members of this set are words that necessarily combine with other words.[5]

The combinatoric property of *eccam* is more complex than mere concatenation or compounding: such a form may combine with an expression that follows at some distance, ignoring intervening material. Included in this class are the infinitive, conjunctive participle, conditional, and adnominal participles. The class of *eccam* 'non-finite verb' is further divided into two smaller sets according to whether the non-finite verb combines with a following noun or verb. The first subset is called *peyareccam* 'adnominal participle', or 'non-finite verb (*eccam*) that combines with a noun (*peyar*)'. The *peyareccam* need not combine directly with its head noun, but may be separated from it by an intervening demonstrative or, in the case of stacked relative clauses, an entire relative clause. In this way it is distinguished from simple compounds of a verb root and noun, e.g. from a compound such as *kol-yāṉai* 'killer elephant' which derives from *kol-* 'kill' and *yāṉai* 'elephant'.

The second subset of *eccam* is called *viṉaiyeccam*, or 'non-finite verb forms that combine with a verb (*viṉai*)'. It includes the infinitive, conjunctive participle, and conditional form, all of which have been amply illustrated. A *viṉaiyeccam* is traditionally said to be "completed" when it combines with a following verb root or, in exceptional circumstances, a predicate nominal. The process of combining with a following verb root is recursive so that indefinitely many *viṉaiyeccam* may appear in a construction. The process is only brought to a stop when a *muṟṟuviṉai* 'finite verb' or predicate nominal completes the sentence.

The term *muṟṟeccam* 'finite verb that functions as a non-finite verb' denotes the set of *muṟṟuviṉai* 'finite verbs' that function as *viṉaiyeccam* 'non-finite verb that combines with a verb'. It identifies any finite verb form that functions as a *viṉaiyeccam*: it identifies all the components of a SVF except the finite verb that appears in the position specially designated for finite predicates. In this way the term *muṟṟeccam* can be used to describe the SVFs in (46) or (51) with equal facility. But since the definition of *muṟṟeccam* incorporates as it were the definition of *viṉaiyeccam*, use of the term *muṟṟeccam* implies the existence of a following verb form which syntactically completes it: this verb form could easily be the one that occupies the specially designated position. Thus, the terms we have introduced so far could be used fully to describe what we call the SVF.

Although the text o *tolkāppiyam* does not use the term *murreccam*, it clearly discusses the phenomenon in *collatikāram* 204.

(55)	...*ceyku*	*eṉ*	*kiḷavi*	*viṉai-(y) oṭu*
	ceyku	say-adnp	expression	verb-soc
	muṭi-(y) iṉ-um		*av-viyal*	*tiri-(y) ātu*...
	complete-cond-and		that nature	deviate-neg-3sn

'Even if an expression of the form *ceyku* is completed, i.e. followed, by another verb, it will not be a deviation in use'.

The verb form *ceyku* 'I will do, make' cited in this sutra is a finite verb form, the first person singular future tense form of *ceyya* 'do, make'. It stands metonymously for all finite verb forms that function as *muṟṟeccam*. This sutra permits verbs of the form *ceyku* to be followed by other verbs in the same syntactic structure without violating Tamil usage. It describes (50)e perfectly. Since the first person singular future tense form *ceyku* occupies a relatively marked cell of the paradigm in virtue of the categories it encodes, it is reasonable to assume that sutra 204 describes other SVFs with less marked finite verb forms. The data above readily support this assumption. Although the text of sutra 204 does not itself employ the term *muṟṟeccam*, the medieval commentator *cēṉāvaraiyar* uses it in his commentary. There he introduces other examples of SVFs, not just those that contain *ceyku* forms. Therefore, sutra 204 and its commentatorial tradition give proof positive of the recognition accorded to the SVF in traditional Tamil grammar.

3. KOTA AND TODA

The Kota and Toda languages, spoken on the Nilgiri plateau, preserve in their past negative conjugations the remnants of a SVF. To see precisely how these conjugations descend from an earlier SVF, extensive comparison should be made with their cognate paradigms in Classical Tamil, Old Telugu, Muṛia Goṇḍi, and Koṇḍa (Steever 1987). The present discussion is limited to the past negative in Kota, but much of what is said applies with equal force to the Toda cognates. The reason behind this limitation is purely heuristic: Kota phonology has not deviated from its Proto-Dravidian source as radically as Toda, so its forms are more easily compared with their cognates in the sister languages. The reader will find the corresponding Toda forms in Emeneau (1984: 145, 169), and may attempt the comparison himself.

The past negative conjugation in Kota is an auxiliary compound verb that consists of the negative stem of the main verb and the past affirmative of the auxiliary verb *āg-*, *āy-* 'become' (Emeneau 1946: 28). Each verb in Kota has two stems, S^1 and S^2, upon which all inflected forms are based. S^2 serves as the basis for the past affirmative, the present-future affirmative, and several other forms; S^1, on the other hand, serves as the base for the corresponding negative forms. The tenseless negative conjugation, which is counted as a finite verb form, consists of S^1 and the appropriate personal ending, e.g., *vār-ē (n)* 'I did/do/will not come' consists of the S^1 *vār-* 'come' and the personal ending *-ē(n)* which marks the first person singular. It is to be positively compared with the Classical Tamil form *vār-ēṉ* 'I did/do/will not come'. Emeneau (1946: 28) observes that, "corresponding to the potential, the irrealis, the future, and the voluntative, negatives are made by adding to S^1 the appropriate forms of the verb *āg-*, *āy-* 'become'; there is also a past made on this pattern, S^1 and the past tense of the same verb." The form *vār-āypē(n)* 'I did not come' consists of the S^1 *vār-* 'come' and the first person singular past affirmative of *āg-*, *āy-* 'become', *āypē(n)* 'I became'. The choice of S^1 in a construction is largely, if not wholly, governed by the presence of the negative morpheme.

The internal structure of the Kota past negative can be graphically represented by the following word-formation rule:[6]

Past Negative *VB+Neg* ⧣ *āy-+Pst Tns+PE.* On the basis of comparative evidence from a number of languages below, the form *vār-āypē (n)* 'I did not come' can be shown to descend from a pre-Kota SVF, **vār-ē(n) āypē (n)* 'I did not come', which is an auxiliary compound verb that consists of the tenseless negative of the main verb and the past affirmative of the auxiliary *āg-*, *āy-*, both verbs being marked for congruent personal endings. This SVF is characterized by the word-formation rule: *Past Negative:* ⧣ *VB+Neg+PE*^{1} ⧣ ⧣*āy-+Pst Tns+PE*^{1}—. A rule of AFFIX-TRUNCATION (see Koṇḍa) eliminates the redundant personal ending on the main verb, creating the attested forms in modern Kota. The rule of Affix-Truncation has much the same effect as the non-application of Rule (45), as we shall see below in greater detail.

The modern Kota forms may be compared with the Classical Tamil negative conjugation in (48): the only difference that separates them is that in Kota the negative morpheme is associated to the main verb through the process of stem alternation while in Classical Tamil it is associated to the auxiliary through the alternation of *al-* 'not become' with *ā-* 'become'. The Kota pattern turns out to be dominant pattern among the sister languages, while the Tamil patterns seems an innovation. Similarly, the reconstructed pre-Kota forms may be favorably compared with the attested Classical Tamil forms in (46), differing only in the exact placement of the negative morpheme. Whereas the alternation between truncated and full forms of the negative conjugation seems to have been a synchronic one in Classical Tamil, the alternation in Kota seems to be diachronic so that pre-Kota has the full SVF while modern Kota has the truncated form.

Ki-Echo Formation in Toda

The discussion of the Kota past negative introduced us to an example of diachronic variation between a fully formed SVF in pre-Kota and a truncated version in the modern language. This comparison with Tamil demonstrated that while one language may lack SVFs, it may by means of such alternations preserve forms that indicate the presence of SVFs at an earlier stage of the language. Such residual forms prove to be as important as genuine SVFs in establishing the presence of the SVF throughout the Dravidian family, and in sanctioning their reconstruction to the proto-language.

While Toda lacks genuine SVFs, it nevertheless has a residual form that alternates comparatively with a SVF in Tamil, pushing back the alternation between full and truncated forms of a SVF to the Proto-South Dravidian era. This form is a variation of the *kI*-echo compound verb already discussed in Tamil. The Toda cognate is a truncated SVF, the Tamil form a full SVF. The specific details of Toda *ki*-Echo Formation may be found in Emeneau (1938a, 1938b, 1939, 1940). As in Tamil, *ki*-Echo Formation in Toda applies in negatives prohibitions, questions, and modal contexts. It applies equally to verbs and nouns. Unlike Tamil, Emeneau (1938a) observes that while *ki*-echo formation applies among nouns to fully inflected forms, when it applies among verbs, "the rules for making the forms are the same as for nouns, but they apply not to the completed forms, but to the stem only." It creates a plan compound verb in which the echoed verb, on which the entire compound is built, appears in its S² form, while the echo word is fully inflected. The following examples make use of the auxiliary *fiḍ-* 'leave', a cognate of Tamil *viṭa* 'leave'; its use indicates that an action is carried out against prior expectations (see Steever 198)3, and is called the 'adversative' (advs) here.

(56)(a) *o·n* *poyk* *fu(k)-kik-fiḍ-eni.*
I-nom dairy-dat enter-*ki*-advs-pres-1s
'I wouldn't enter the dairy or do any such thing.'

(b) *o·n* *al* *iθ-xiθ-fiḍ-eni.*
I-nom there remain-*kI*-advs-pres-1s
'I won't remain there or do any such thing.'

(c) *al* *θid̲-xid̲-fi-c-a·?*
there eat-*ki*-advs-pst-2s-int
'Did you eat there or do any such (polluting) thing?'

(d) *poyk* *fu(k)-kik-fi-c-a·?*
daiy-dat enter-*ki*-advs-pst-2s-int
'Did you enter the dairy or do any such (polluting) thing?'

Consider the first example (56) a. The morphological structure of *fukikfiḍeni* 'I wouldn't enter the dairy or do any such thing' is analyzed as the verb base *fuk-* 'enter', the *ki*-echo form *-kik-*, the adversative auxiliary *fiḍ-* 'leave', and the pormanteau morph *-eni* which marks both the present-future tense and agreement with a first person singular subject. The echoed verb bases in (56) b and c end in consonants which spirantize the intial *k* of *ki* to *x*. What is important here is that the echo verb, compounded with the adversative auxiliary, bears the finite inflections while the echoed verb appears in its S[2] form. This *ki*-echo compound structurally resembles the plain compound verbs of Classical Tamil in (48) and (52)c-f, where the main verb appears in its bare base form while the auxiliary is inflected. These Tamil forms appear to have alternated with full SVFs at the same time in the same language. The structural alternation between the Tamil *ki*-echo compounds in (54)b and the Toda cognates in (56) is identical except that the SVF occurs in one language while the corresponding plain compound verb occurs in a sister language. On the strength of such parallels, one can reconstruct the alternation between SVFs and plain compound verbs in the negative conjugation and the *ki*-echo compound to Proto-South Dravidian. Evidence presented below from Kolami gives us reason to project this alternation even further back into the past.

4. KANNAḌA

Although grammars of Old Kannaḍa do not generally recognize the presence of SVFs in the language, certain collocations in the *vikramārjuna vijaya*, popularly known as *pāmpa bhārata*, lend themselves to interpretation as SVFs.

(57)(a) *sugid(u)* *ōḍ-id-ar* *all-ar-ē* *kā-v-ar*. (11.125)
fear-cp run-pst-3p become-neg-3p-emp guard-fut-3p
'They did not run away in fear; they guarded (them).'

(b) *gel-v-uv(u)* *all-avu.* (6.67)
win-fut-3p become-neg-3p
'They will not win.'

(c) *mīru-v-ar* *all-ar.* (4.7)
transgress-fut-3p become-neg-3p
'They will not transgress.'

Such collocations of finite verb form and a form of *al-* 'not become' inflected for congruent personal endings are usually interpreted as a finite verb followed by a tag-question, perhaps on the analogy of the tag-question marker *allavā* 'isn't it so?' in the modern language. Thus the collocation *ōḍidar allar* in (57)a is conventionally interpreted as, 'They ran away, didn't they?'. It is not clear that the contexts of these colloctions can ultimately sustain this kind of interpretation. An alternative reading, based on clear structural parallels with the Tamil negative conjugation in (46), glosses them as members of a negative SVF. So strong and compelling is the outward resemblance between the Kannaḍa forms in (57) and the Tamil counterparts in (46) that comparative methodology requires us to treat them as cognates with the same semantic interpretation, until contrary evidence surfaces. Further examples appear in *vikramārjuna vijaya* 6.53, 8.56, and 11.122. I suspect that intensive comparison with their Tamil cognates will support our claim that they belong to a negative conjugation. More to the point, however, is the fact that whatever their proper semantic interpretation may ultimately be, their syntactic analysis is unambiguous. These Kannaḍa collocations clearly satisfy our definition of the SVF because both members are formally finite verbs in a single compound verb construction. Even if *allar* 'they do not become' in (57)a is created through the application of TAG-QUESTION FORMATION to *ōḍidar* 'they ran', the resulting compound *ōḍidar allar* has the internal structure of a compound verb, not a complex sentence. Old Kannaḍa therefore has SVFs.

Medieval Kannaḍa

Study of the *vīraśaiva* literature turns up a number of lexical compound verbs which are formally SVFs. These SVFs are iterative compounds in which a finite verb is reduplicated to signal the repetition or intensity of an action. Consider the two following examples, the first from *basavaṇṇa*, the second from *akkamahādēvi*.

(58) (a) *nān* *ē-v-en* *ē-v-en* *ayya.*
I-nom beg-fut-1s beg-fut-1s lord-oc
'O lord, I continually entreat (you).'

(b) *embattunālku* *lakṣa* *yōniyoḷage* *ba-nd-e* *ba-nd-e.*
eighty-four 100,000 vagina-loc come-pst-1s come-pst-1s
'I have repeatedly come (to rebirth) through eighty-four hundred thousand vaginas.'

Much the same pattern perdures in modern Kannaḍa, where the phrase *bande bande* 'I am coming right now' signals through reduplication a pressing urgency that the single finite verb *bande* 'I came, am coming' does not have by itself.[7] The reduplicated finite verbs in (58) satisfy the definition of the SVF.

Within this same corpus may be found an alternative means of signaling iteration or intensity of an action through the use of reduplication. Unlike the examples in (58), here only the bare verb base is reduplicated, and only the last component of the resulting compound bears inflections.

(59)(a) *ānanda-(d) inda* *nali-nali-d(u)* *āduve.*
joy-instr dance-dance-cp become-fut-1s
'I will dance and dance for joy.'

(b) *ānanda-(d) inda* *kuni-kuni-d(u)* *āduve.*
joy-instr jump-jump-cp become-fut-1s
'I will jump and jump for joy.'

In (59)a the compound verb *nalidu āduve* 'I will dance' serves as the basis of the reduplicated compound *nali-nalidu āduve* 'I will dance and dance' in which only the verb base *nali-* 'dance' is repeated. Such forms also exist in the modern language, e.g., *nagu-tt-āre* 'they laugh' is reduplicated as *nagu-nagu-ttāre* 'they laugh and laugh' by copying only the bare verb base *nagu-* 'laugh'. The alternation between the iterative compounds in (58) and (59) resembles other alternations that we have already seen to occur between a SVF and plain compound verb. The variants may be related by Rule (45): its application creates a SVF, its non-application a plain compound verb.

Gi-Echo Formation

A cognate of the Tamil and Toda *ki*-echo compound formations, the Kannaḍa *gi*-echo compound formation functions in much the same way. Some minor differences naturally exist. If the word to be echoed begins in *gi-* or *gī-*, the echo word begins with *pa-* or *pā-*. Conditions on its application are broader than those seen so far inasmuch as an echo compound occasionally appears in the past tense.

(60) (a) *amerikakke hōgu-tt-āne gīgu-tt-āne and-are*
America-dat go-pres-3sm *gi*-pres-3sm say-cond
namage kaṣṭa.
we-dat trouble-nom
'If he goes to America or does any such thing, it will be difficult for us.'

(b) *alli hōgu gīgu, ninage sariyāgi sikṣa āgatte.*
there go-imp gi-imp you-dat properly punishment get-pres-3sn
'If you go there or do any such thing, you'll be properly punished.'

(c) *cikkappana biṭṭu giṭṭu ellādarū hōd-īye gīd-īye.*
uncle-acc leave-cp *gi*-cp anywhere go-cnt-2s *gi*-cnt-2s
'(Be careful lest) you might be separated from your uncle or something, you might go off somewhere or do some such thing.'

(61)(a) *ī kaḍe tale hāk-īya.*
this place head put-cnt-2s
'Don't (dare) show your face here!'

(b) *ī kaḍe tale hāk-gik-īya.*
this place head put-*gi*-cnt-2s
'Don't (dare) show you face here or do anything like it !'

A straightforward comparison may be made between the Tamil *ki*-echo compound in (54)b and the Kannaḍa cognate in (60)a: in both a SVF is embedded by the conditional form of a FPEP. The SVF in (60)b, *hōgu gīgu* 'if you go or do any such thing', is based on the imperative form *hōgu* 'go'. Accompanied by a rising intonation the finite imperative functions as the non-finite conditional: its presence signals a stern warning or challenge (see note 23, Chapter I). Another finite verb form in Kannaḍa, the contingent (cnt), may be reduplicated by means of *gi*-echo formation. Here, however, two different outputs may occur. In (60)c the echoed word *hōdīye* '(lest) you might go' is completely echoed, resulting in the SVF *hōdīye gīdīye* '(lest) you might go or do some such thing'. This is to be compared with (61) b where the echo compound formation *hāk-gik-iya* '(lest) you might put or do some such thing' is the result of echoing only the bare verb base of the echoed word, not the entire inflected form as in (61) a (see Bright 1958: 28). Here is more evidence for an alternation between a plain compound verb and a SVF within a single language, not between two different languages.

KOḌAGU

Although I have not made a thorough study of the language, preliminary field-work on Koḍagu reveals the presence of SVFs in the form of *gi*-echo compound verbs. The two examples below conform to the pattern of echo compounds that is beginning to emerge from our survey.

	ava	*cō-p-a*	*gī-p-a*	*endī*	*gottille.*
(62) (a)	he-nom	lose-fut-3sm	*gi*-fut-3sm	say-cp	know-neg
	'I don't know whether he will lose or what he will do.'				

	kuḍippakī	*giḍippakī*	*koḍ-ate*	*giḍ-ate.*
(b)	drink-vn-dat	*gi*-vn-dat	give-neg-imp	*gi*-neg-imp
	'Don't give him anything to drink, or do any such thing.'			

According to our definition, both *cōpa gīpa* 'he will lose or do something' in (62)a and *koḍate giḍate* 'don't give him or do any such thing' in (62)b are full-fledged SVFs, generated by *gi*-echo formation.

6. SUMMARY

Evidence from Tamil, Kannaḍa, and Koḍagu confirms the presence of the SVF in South Dravidian. Classical Tamil in particular shows a wide variety of SVFs including both auxiliary and lexical compound verbs in its repetory. Moreover, traditional Tamil grammarians acknowledge their presence and provide a terminology for their analysis. Kota and Toda preserve the remnants of a negative conjugation which, on the basis of comparison with South-Central Dravidian, can be shown to descend from an earlier SVF. It is suggested below that the so-called past tense form with the inflectional increment *-aṉ-* in Classical Tamil is in fact the contracted residue of an earlier SVF which signaled the present perfect tense (see Pengo). Even so, the SVF is clearly moribund in South Dravidian: it tends to be lost in historical development, as the transition from Classical Tamil into Modern Tamil and Malayāḷam attests. The substitution of SVFs with plain compound verbs largely coincides with the loss of Rule (45) and rules that inflect predicate nominals for agreement with their subjects.

Only the echo compound and, to a lesser extent, the iterative compounds continue to provide South Dravidian with SVFs. The processes of Echo Compound Formation and Reduplication which create *ki*-echo compounds and iterative compounds, respectively, are both distinct from Rule (45) because neither one has to specify the lexical category of its operands, Nouns and verbs alike, inflected for a wide variety of grammatical categories can be echoed and reduplicated. It is only when these processes apply to a finite verb that they give rise to a SVF. The fact that such compounds persist in South Dravidian is strong evidence that the grammars of these languages, particularly their individual versions of Rule (44), permit the creation and preservation of SVFs, even if on a limited scale.

Chapter Four

SERIAL VERBS IN SOUTH-CENTRAL DRAVIDIAN

1. TELUGU

THE language of Old Telugu, particularly as it is preserved in the *nannayya mahābhārata* (c. AD 1200), possesses a negative conjugation whose members are formally SVFs. As illustrated in Table 1, each cell of the past negative paradigm is occupied by a SVF whose two component forms are on independent grounds finite forms. The main verb appears in the "tenseless" negative, the auxiliary verb *agu*, 'become' (*DEDR* 333) appears in the past affirmative, and both are inflected with congruent personal endings. The form *ceppan*(*u*) *aytini* 'I did not say' consists, therefore, of *cepp-anu* 'I do not say' and *ay-t-ini* 'I became'. The remaining cells of the paradigm have an identical analysis. Comparison shows us that this form is cognate with the past negative paradigms in Kota, Toda, Muria Gonḍi, Konḍa, and, perhaps, Kolami.

TABLE 1: The Past Negative SVF of *ceppa* 'say' in Old Telugu

	Singular	Plural
1	*ceppan*(*u*) *aytini*	*ceppam*(*u*) *aytimi*
2	*ceppaw*(*u*) *aytiwi*	*ceppar*(*u*) *aytiri*
3m	*ceppaḍ*(*u*) *ayye*(*n*)	*ceppar*(*u*) *ayiri*
3n	*ceppad*(*u*) *ayye*(*n*)	*ceppaw*(*u*) *ayye*(*n*)

Modern Telugu

Although the SVF is restricted in Modern Telugu, its presence in modern dialects has been recorded by Arden (1937: 160, 166), P. S. Subrahmanyam (1971: 351), and Krishnamurti and Gwynn (1985: 178). Note that all of these examples are auxiliary compound verbs that convey negation.

(63)(a) *koṭṭut-unn-ānu* *kā-nu.*
strike-pres-1s become-neg-1s
'I am not striking.'

(b) *nēnu cēs-in-ānu* *kā-nu.*
I-nom do-pst-1s become-neg-1s
'I did not do.'

(c) *nēnu* *ninna* *veḷḷ-ǣ-nu* *kā-nu* (~*kā-du*).
I-nom yesterday go-pst-1s become-neg-1s (~become-neg-3sn)
'I did not go yesterday.'

(d) *vaḷḷu* *monna* *cepp-ǣ-ru* *kā-ru* (~*kā-du*).
they-nom d-b-y tell-pst-3p become-neg-3p (~become-neg-3sn)
'They did not tell me the day before yesterday.'

The negative SVF in (63)a, *koṭṭutunnānu kānu* 'I am not striking', consists of the main verb *koṭṭutunnānu* 'I am striking', inflected for both the present tense and agreement with a first person subject, and the auxiliary verb *kānu* 'I do not become', inflected for negation and a personal ending congruent with the main verb's. The three remaining examples have the same analysis with one qualification: they substitute the past tense marker for the present tense marker, and consequently change the form's meaning to the past negative. There is a tendency for an invariant form of the auxiliary, the third person neuter singular negative *kādu* 'it does not become', to replace all of the other personal forms of the auxiliary in this paradigm, e.g. *kānu* 'I do not become', *kāru* 'you do not become'. Even with this change, these compound verbs still qualify as SVFs because each of their components is on independent grounds a finite verb form.[1] Comparison of these forms with their predecessors in Old Telugu reveals a historical change: the negative morpheme is now associated with the auxiliary whereas it was formerly incorporated into the main verb. When we compare these two paradigms with their cognates in other languages, we can according to their distribution conclude that the past negative paradigm in Old Telugu, Gonḍi, and Konḍa is the original, and that the corresponding paradigms in Old Tamil and Modern Telugu are the innovators.

The negative counterfactual conditional in Modern Telugu seems also to be a SVF. The only trouble with this interpretation is the fact that the counterfactual conditional (cfc) form historically descends from a verbal noun inflected for agreement with its subject, and not from a finite verb. There are two arguments in favor of interpreting it as a verb, not a verbal noun. It tends to replace the old aorist, a finite verb form, in its function as a marker of the apodosis of a counterfactual conditional. Second, the specialized meaning it has acquired in this function cannot be predicted from the meaning of the verbal noun from which it has descended. That verbal noun has a habitual meaning, not a counterfactual conditional one. These two considerations persuade me that this form, despite its nominal origin, is rapidly becoming a finite verb form, if in fact it has not already done so.

(64)(a) *āyana* *aḍigi-tē,* *nēnu* *cepp-ēwāṇ-ṇi.*
he-nom ask-cond I-nom tell-cfc-1s
'If he (had) asked, I would have told him.'

(b) *āyana* *aḍigi-tē,* *nēnu* *cepp-ēwāṇ-ṇi* *kā-nu.*
he-non ask-cond I-nom tell-cfc-1s become-neg-1s
'If he (had) asked, I would not have told him.'

(c) *mīru* *mā* *iṇṭi-ki* *was-tē,* *mīku* *bhōjanam*
you-nom our house-dat come-cond you-dat food
peṭṭ-ēwāḷḷ-am.
give-cfc-1p
'If you had come to our house, we would have given you food.'

(d) *mīru* *mā* *iṇṭi-ki* *was-tē,* *mīku* *bhōjanam*
you-nom our house-dat come-cond you-dat food
peṭṭ-ēwāḷḷ-am *kā-mu.*
give-cfc-1p become-neg-1p
'If you had come to our house, we would not have given you food.'

As in the examples in (63)c and d, the personal forms of the auxiliary verb alternate with the invariant form *kādu* 'it does not become'. These SVFs seem to be unstable in the modern language, and therefore likely targets for historical change. On the one hand, both the dialectal variation of these examples and their tendency to replace the personal forms of the auxiliary verb with a single, invariant negative marker, undermining their status as SVFs, suggest that these forms may lapse into total disuse. On the other hand, the fact that this pattern now occurs in the present, past, and counterfactual conditional negative paradigms favorably argues for a progressive expansion of the use of the SVF throughout the history of Telugu. Gonḍi provides us with a much more dramatic example of such expansion, the result of which is that virtually any finite verb form in Gonḍi has a corresponding negative SVF form.

Iterative and Echo Compounds

Bhaskararao's (1977: 5) study of reduplication in Telugu gives evidence of the existence of iterative SVFs.

(65) (a) *cūs-t-ānu* *cūs-t-ānu.*
see-fut-1s see-fut-1s
'I shall continue seeing for sometime.'

(b) *cūs-ē-nu* *cūs-ē-nu.*
see-pst-1s see-pst-1s
'I continued seeing for some time.'

The iterative SVF *cūstānu cūstānu* 'I shall continue seeing' in (65)a is based on the single finite verb *cūstānu* 'I shall see', similarly *cūsēnu cūsēnu* 'I continued seeing' is based on the finite *cūsēnu* 'I saw'. Bhaskararao observes that such reduplication occurs only in the future and past affirmative forms, not in their negative counterparts.

gi-echo compound formation in Modern Telugu may apply to finite verbs in affective contexts such as questions, negatives, and modals to create a SVF. This process is clearly cognate with the other echo compound processes we have already seen, but some minor variation exists. The *gi*-echo compound has a distributive meaning, but it does not always exhibit the pejorative sense that its Tamil cognate does. In this respect the Telugu *gi*-echo compound tends to behave more and more like balance compounds, of which we shall see more later. If the word to be echoed begins in *gi*- or *gī*-, the echo word begins in *pi*- or *pī*-.

(66) (a) *cēs -æ-ḍ-ā* *gīs-æ-ḍ-ā*?
do-pst-3sm-int *gi*-pst-3sm-int
'Did he work or (do) anything?' 'He didn't work at all.'

(b) *vinṭ-ā-ḍ-ā* *ginṭ-ā-ḍ-ā*?
hear-pst-3sm-int *gi*-pst-3sm-int
'Did he hear or take any notice?' 'He didn't hear at all.'

(c) *cepp-anu* *gipp-anu.*
tell-neg-1s *gi*-neg-1s
'I won't tell or do anything like that.'

(d) *wāḍu* *ceppa* *lēdu* *gippa* *lēdu.*
he-nom tell-inf be-neg-3sn *gi*-inf be-neg-3sn
'He didn't tell or do anything like that.'

The four SVFs in (66) are *gi*-echo compounds that are based on the finite verb forms *cēsæḍu* 'he worked', *vinṭāḍu* 'he heard', *ceppanu* 'I will not tell', and *ceppa lēdu* 'did not tell', respectively. Note that the basis of the echo compound in (66)d, *ceppa lēdu* 'did not tell', is itself a compound verb every detail of which is echoed in the final compound verb.

Related Forms and Rules

The presence of the SVF in a language, it has been proposed, implies the existence elsewhere in that language of other structures and processes that seem to be components of Rule (45). The SVF seems to thrive wherever we find plain compound verbs based on the bare verb base of the first component, and a rule to inflect predicate nominals for agreement with their subjects, corresponding roughly to the structural description and the structural change of Rule (45). Both of these components are found in Telugu.

(67) (a) *nēnu* *bīdavaṇ-ṇi.*
I-nom poor man-nom-1s
'I am a poor man.'

(b) *nīvu* *guḍḍivāḍa-vu.*
you-nom blind man-nom-2s
'You are a blind man.'

(c) *nēnu* *brahmaṇuḍa-nu* *kā-nu.*
I-nom brahmin-nom-1s become-neg-1s
'I am not a brahmin.'

(d) *mēmu* *pilla-l-amu* *kā-mu.*
we-nom children-nom-1p become-neg-1p
'We are not children'

The Telugu examples in (67)c and d are to be positively compared with the Tamil example in (49)c. For reasons stated in note 1, Chapter III we cannot assimilate such examples to the set of SVFs, but must content ourselves with viewing them as related phenomena whose presence buoys up that of the SVF.

Telugu also has compound verb formations whose first member appears in its bare base form. The Old Telugu compound *ē-tencu* 'come' is derived from the bare verb base of *ē-/egu* 'go' (*DEDR* 871) and an inflected form of *tencu-/teccu* 'give to you or me' (*DEDR* 3098). In the modern language reflexive compound verbs may be formed by "suffixing" an inflected form of the verb *konu* 'hold, take' (*DEDR* 2151) to the bare base of a verb (see Arden 1937: 152). Thus, Telugu has a construction that is known in other languages, e.g. Tamil, Kannaḍa, to alternate with SVFs through the application of Rule (45), or the lack of it. These two grammatical phenomenon help to support the existence of SVFs in Telugu in three forms: the negative conjugation, iterative compounds, and *gi*-echo compounds.

2. MURIA GONḌI

According to the *Census of India* 1971, Gonḍi is spoken by 1,500,000 people in numerous dialects scattered over the four states of Maharashtra, Madhya Pradesh, Andhra Pradesh, and Orissa. Even though Gonḍi has been recognized as a Dravidian language for the past century, it has been fragmentarily and inadequately described due in large part to the diversity of dialects. However, with Andres' (1977) grammar of Muria Gonḍi, spoken in the Bastar district of Madhya Pradesh, this lamentable situation has been put aright. Her grammar of Muria Gonḍi stands heads and shoulders above everything else written on any dialect of the language, and shows us the direction which future Gonḍi studies might profitably take. All the examples of SVFs in Gonḍi have been taken from her grammar, so that what is said about the language here must be understood as pertaining only to this one dialect.

The Negative Conjugation

Andres (1977) records within the larger negative conjugation five separate paradigms, all of which are formally expressed as SVFs. The overall structure of the SVF is the same for all five: the main verb has the form of the tenseless negative, the auxiliary verb marks tense, aspect, or mood, and both verbs are inflected for congruent personal endings. Each component of the SVF is a finite verb in its own right. These SVFs are considered first in example sentences, then in tabulated paradigms. (The diacritic ' in the examples marks a phonologically relevant boundary.)

(68) (a) *uṟ'-on* *an'-d-an.*
watch-neg-1s be-pst impf-1s
'I wasn't watching.'

(b) *punn-on* *a-t-an.*
known-neg-1s become-pst-1s
'I didn't know.'

(c) *loh'k* *here* *avv-tekkeṅ* *naNd'-oR*
house-pl some reach-cond get wet-neg-3sm
ay'-eR.
become-subj-3sm
'If he reached some houses, he would not get wet.'

(d) *nima* *va-t-i* *aske,* *mavaṅ* *polloyiṅ*
you-nom come-pst-2s when our language
punn-vi *a-t-i.*
know-neg-2s become-pst-2s
'When you came, you did not know our language.'

The compound verb *punnon atan* 'I didn't know' in (68)b is a SVF because both of its component parts are independently finite verb forms: *punnon* 'I do not know' and *atan* 'I did not become'. The three other examples share the same overall structure, differing only in the identity of the morpheme for tense, aspect, or mood incorporated in the main verb.

The six following paradigms, from Andres (1977: 559, pass.), illustrate in tabular form the various negative finite forms of the verb *oll-* 'bend over'. The first paradigm exhibits the forms of the simple, tenseless negative, which occurs as a component in the five remaining paradigms.

TABLE 2: The Simple Tenseless Negative, *oll-* 'bend over', Gonḍi.

	Singular	Plural
1	*oll'on*	*oll'om* (excl) *ollval* (incl)
2	*ollvi*	*ollvir*
3m	*oll'oR*	*oll'or*
3n	*oll'o*	*oll'oṅ*

TABLE 3: The Perfective Past Negative, *oll-* 'bend over' Goṇḍi.

	Singular	Plural
1	*oll'on atan*	*oll'om atom* (excl) *ollval atal* (incl)
2	*ollvi ati*	*ollvir atir*
3m	*oll'oR atoR*	*oll'or atur*
3n	*oll'o atu*	*oll'oṅ atuṅ*

TABLE 4: The Imperfective Negative Past, *oll-* 'bend over', Goṇḍi.

	Singular	Plural
1	*oll'on an'dan*	*oll'om an'dom* (excl) *ollval an'dal* (incl)
2	*ollvi an'di*	*ollvir an'dir*
3m	*oll'oR an'doR*	*oll'or an'dur*
3n	*oll'o an'du*	*oll'oṅ an'duṅ*

TABLE 5: The Imperfective Nonpast Negative, *oll-* 'bend over', Goṇḍi

	Singular	Plural
1	*oll'on an'tonan*	*oll'om an'torom* (excl) *ollval an'tolal* (incl)
2	*ollvi an'tun*	*ollvir an'torir*
3m	*oll'oR an'toR*	*oll'or an'tor*
3n	*oll'o an'ta*	*oll'oṅ an'taṅ*

TABLE 6: The Predictive Negative, *oll-* 'bend over', Goṇḍi.

	Singular	Plural
1	*oll'on ay'kan*	*oll'om ay'kom* (excl) *ollval ay'kal* (incl)
2	*ollvi ay'ki*	*ollvir ay'kir*
3m	*oll'oR ay'noR*	*oll'or ay'nur*
3n	*oll'o ayaR*	*oll'oṅ ay'nuṅ*

TABLE 7: The Subjunctive Negative, *oll-* 'bend over', Goṇḍi.

	Singular	Plural
1	*oll'on ay'enan*	*oll'om ay'erom* (excl) *ollval ay'elal* (incl)
2	*ollvi ay'en*	*ollvir ay'eri1*
3m	*oll'oR ay'eR*	*oll'or ay'er*
3n	*oll'o ay'val*	*oll'on ay'vas* (*k*)

Consider Table 2 where the first person singular of the simple tenseless negative verb *oll'on* means 'I didn't/don't/won't bend over'. The corresponding form in Table 3, the perfective past negative, is *oll'on atan* 'I did not bend over'; in Table 4, the imperfective past negative, *oll'on an'dan* 'I was not bending over'; in Table 5, the imperfective nonpast negative, *oll'on an' tonan* 'I am not bending over'; in Table 6, the predictive negative, *oll'on ay'kan* 'I will not bend over'; and in Table 7, the subjunctive negative, *oll'on ay'enan* 'I would not bend over/would not have bent over'. Each cell of every paradigm from Table 3 to Table 7 is occupied by a SVF. Note that the Muria Goṇḍi forms in Table 3 are perfect cognates of the Old Telugu forms in Table 1: they correspond morpheme for morpheme. The reconstructed forms of the past negative in Kota, Toda, and Koṇḍa (see below) also correspond exactly to the morphemic structure of these two paradigms: all are SVFs that signal the past negative.

Muria Goṇḍi does not appear to have any other SVFs apart from these five paradigms. Andres (1977: 154, note) observes the limited distribution of SVFs, and offers a partial explanation for it when she remarks that "an auxiliary verb marked for tense may occur along with the negative verb in a single phrase, whereas two tensed verbs do not normally appear together in a single phrase." Although the simple tenseless verb satisfies the syntactic criterion for finiteness, Andres' observation captures the valuble insight that, morphologically considered, the tenseless negative form is somehow "less finite" than one that overtly marks tense and subject-verb agreement. Such verb forms define the "prototypical" finite verb, one which stands at the core of all finite verb forms. The tenseless negative lies on the periphery of this set because it does not mark the prototypically characteristic morpheme of tense. Any historical change that brings about the loss of SVFs is essentially a morphological one involving the loss of the rule that copies the morphological features of one verb onto another. It stands to reason that the prototypical finite verb will bear the brunt of such a change while the more peripheral forms will be less severely affected, and will tend to last longer in the language. Not only has the negative SVF persisted in Muria Goṇḍi, but the number of negative paradigms has grown proportionally with the development of new finite paradigms in the affirmative. The Telugu and

Goṇḍi data might easily lead one to suspect that a number of these negative SVFs could be reconstructed to Proto-South-Central Dravidian.

Related Forms and Rules

Muria Goṇḍi has the two related grammatical phenomena that seem to accompany SVFs wherever they occur. It has compound verbs that utilize the bare verb base, and it has rules that inflect predicate nominals for agreement with their subjects. The bare verb base, which is the same as the infinitive in Goṇḍi (Andres 1977: 195), is a free form that appears in a wide variety of constructions.

(69) (a) *accoḍahk* *parhk* *ann' oR.*
then-abl look-bvb go-neg-3sm
'Since then he hasn't gone to look (for a wife).'

(b) *cahha* *unḍa* *vay'lerom.*
tea drink-bvd come-subj-1pin
'We had come (earlier) to drink tea.'

(c) *likkah* *kiya* *mand'aR.*
writing do-bvb be-prd-3n
'She will stay to write.'

(d) *naNgedun* *puh* *tattak* *indana.*
plow-acc plow-bvb fetch-hrt say-vn
'One should say, "Fetch the plow to plow." '

The forms *parhk* 'look for', *unḍa* 'drink', *kiya* 'do', and *puh* 'plow' in these examples are bare verb bases that combine with a following inflected verb. These constructions do not alternate with SVFs, nor, on the other hand, do the SVFs above alternate with plain compound verbs, but the grammar of Muria Goṇḍi preserves both structures even though the alternation has lapsed from the language. The Goṇḍi examples in (69) may be favorably compared with the Tamil examples in (52) c-f, where the bare verb base combines with a following verb that denotes simple motion. The Goṇḍi verbs *vaya* 'come' in (69) b and *tatta* 'fetch' in (69) d are cognates of the Tamil verbs *vara* 'come' in (52)e-f and *tara* 'give to you or me' in (52) c-d. And these Tamil plain compound verbs do appear to alternate with SVFs in (50) and (51).

Like the other dialects of the language, Muria Goṇḍi has a feature-copying rule that marks agreement between a subject and a predicate nominal or a predicate adjective. Goṇḍi seems to have generalized this pattern from one of derivation to one of inflection (see Kurylowicz 1964: 35, pass.) so that adjectives and substantives in attributive position also mark agreement. The pattern seems to have been generalized from the predicate position of the sentence. Some examples of this agreement phenomenon are presented here, but a full exposition is beyond the scope of this book and the curious reader should refer to the pertinent sections of Andres (1977). Since it is not clear to what extent nouns and adjectives are distinct categories in this language, the presence of various labels such as 'nom' for nominative in the glosses is not systematic, but rather heuristic.

(70)(a)	*ivv*	*bata-ṅ*	*kageti-ṅ*?
	this-p-nom	what kind-p-nom	paper-p-nom
	'What kind of papers are these?'		
(b)	*nivaṅ*	*kall-k*	*maliya-s.*
	you-p-nom	hair-p-nom	brown-p-nom
	'Your hairs are brown.' 'Yours are brown hairs.'		
(c)	*or*	*kariyal-or.*	
	they-p-nom	black-p-nom	
	'Those men are dark-skinned.'		
(d)	*ikkeḍ-or*	*leyy-or*	*ann-or.*
	this place-pm-nom	young man-pm-nom	go-neg-3pm
	'The young men of this place won't go.'		

Note that in (70)a the attributive noun *bata* 'what kind' in inflected for the plural marker *-ṅ* to agree with the plural predicate nominal *kagetiṅ* 'papers'. The remaining examples have similar analyses. The rules that are responsible for this kind of agreement resembles Rule (45) in that they also non-contrastively copy features of person, number, and gender onto the components of a construction. The growth of these agreement rules may in fact support the preservation and expansion of the negative SVFs in Gonḍi.

3. KONḌA

Krishnamurti's (1969) grammar and texts of Konḍa provides us with many examples and many varieties of the SVF. The most structurally transparent is the balance compound verb, a lexical compound verb which juxtaposes two semantically similar verbs. In another, highly productive pattern, the component verbs of the SVF mark agreement with the designated finite predicate by means of truncated personal endings rather than full replicas of the personal ending on the designated finite verb. This system descends from earlier SVFs, which must have been widespread in the prehistory of the language. Finally, in the past negative conjugation, the components of an earlier, analytic SVF have fused into a single, synthetic verb form in modern Konḍa. The etymology of this form shows us that the process of truncating non-contrastive personal endings within a SVF plays a central role in the historical development of the past negative. Further comparison with Pengo, Malto, and Kuṛux confirms that this process is an ancient one.

Balance Compound Verbs

No one who reads a traditional grammar of one of the literary languages can fail to appreciate the active and extensive role that compounding has. This is no less true of the non-literary languages. Since most of the Dravidian languages have just verbs and nouns, compound formation provides a means of creating new, complex constructions out of various combinations of these two parts of speech. We have already had the chance to examine iterative compound and echo compounds. Another kind of distributive compound is the BALANCE COMPOUND which consists of two words of the same category and which expresses a general concept of which each member of the compound expresses a specific, typical instance. The Kannaḍa balance compound noun *dana-dhyāna* 'moveable property' consists of *dana* 'cattle' and *dhānya* 'grain'; the Tamil compound verb *āṭiṉir pāṭiṉir* 'you celebrated' in (51)a consists of the two finite verb *āṭiṉir* 'you danced' and *pāṭiṉir* 'you sang'. The Konḍa examples below are balance SVFs.

(71) (a) *vānṟu* *ki-t-i* *palaŋaṟu* *vānṟu*
he-nom do-pst-adnp tooth-stick he-nom
iyba-t-i *ēṟu,*
bathe-pst-adnp water
vānṟu *mū-ṭ-i* *mūlku,* *vizu* *aya* *kulur*
he-nom urinate-pst-adnp urine all that crane
poṭi *ti-n-ad* *u-ṇ-ad* (Text 7.15).
bird-nom eat-npst-3sn drink-npst-3sn
'That crane consumes everything: the tooth-stick that man used, the water he bathed in, and the urine he passed.'

(b) *ādvati* *mēṟa-mide* *āzi* *soniv* (Text 8.382).
next mansion become-cp go-hrt
'Next, let a mansion become mine.'

(c) *mēṟa* *ā-t-ad* *mide*
storied building become-pst-3sn terraced building
ā-t-ad.
become-pst3sn
'A mansion became (his).'

(d) *mēṟa-d* *o-t-ar* *mide-d*
storied building-obl take-pst-3pm terraced building-obl
o-t-ar (Text 8.382).
take-pst-3pm
'They took (away) the mansion.'

(e) *suṭa* *ti-R-an* *pogo* *ti-R-an* (Text 9.105).
cigar smoke-pst-3sm smoke smoke-pst-3sm
'He smoked a cigar.'

The balance SVF *tinad uṇad* 'it consumes' in (71)a consists of the two finite verb *tiṇad* 'it eats' and *unad* 'it drinks'. The other examples do not as readily yield to analysis. The balance compound noun *mēṛa-mide* 'mansion' in (71)b consists of two simple nouns, *mēṛa* 'storied building' and *mide* 'terraced building' (cf. Tamil *māṭa-māḷikai* 'palace'), and is combined with a single finite form of *ā-* 'become'. In the very next sentence of the running text, reproduced in (71)c, this balance compound noun has been split up into its two component parts, each of which is accompanied by a finite form of *ā-* 'become'. Although each half of the resulting balance compound in (71)c consists of one-half of the original balance compound noun and *ātad* 'it became', the whole must still be considered as a compound since the two parts do not refer to distinct entities or actions. It is thus a balance SVF whose individual parts consist of a noun and a finite verb form. Similarly in (71)d, each half of the balance compound noun *mēṛa-mide* 'mansion' combines with an instance of the finite verb *otar* 'they took', so that the whole construction may be considered a SVF whose two component parts each consist of a noun and a finite verb form. Example (71)e follows this same pattern: the balance compound noun *suṭa pogo* 'cigar smoke' has been split into two parts, each of which is accompanied by the finite verb form *tiRan* 'he smoke'. Despite the fact that the component parts of these balance compounds are syntactically complex, containing a noun and a finite verb, the whole compound nevertheless satisfies the definition of the SVF.

The Truncation of Repeated Personal Endings

Koṇḍa has a special family of constructions, the structure of which resembles the internal structure of the SVFs that have already appeared in our catalogue. Like the SVF, this kind of construction consists of two or more verbs that mark concord among themselves by means of repeated, non-contrastive suffixes. Also like the SVF it marks concord by copying the suffix of the rightmost verb—that is, the head of the construction—onto all preceding verbs in the same construction. But unlike the SVF, it copies only a truncated version, and not a full replica of the suffix. All of the verbs within such a construction mark tense, and in all but a circumscribed subset the tense markers must agree. The majority of examples we consider are ones in which the head of the construction occupies the position specially designated for finite predicates, and bears inflections for tense and subject-verb agreement. The relation between the full and truncated versions of a suffix is encapsulated in the following rule: if the personal ending has the shape $-(((V_1)C_1)\,V_2C_2)$, then the truncated form is simply $-V_1$.[2] If, for example, the head verb bears the personal ending *-ider* to mark agreement with a second person plural subject, all of the remaining verbs in the construction have the truncated affix *-i* directly following the tense marker. The process of AFFIX-TRUNCATION seems in certain ways the opposite of Rule (45) because it appears to undo much of what this rule generates. But Affix-Truncation removes only part of the repeated non-contrastive ending, leaving behind a telltale vowel as a reminder of the agreement among the part of the SVFs. Comparative and internal evidence suggest that these TRUNCATED SVFs descend from earlier, full-fledged SVFs through the application of Affix-Truncation in the historical development of Koṇḍa.

The first kind of Truncated SVF, illustrated as a paradigm in Table 8, is not a compound verb but a construction that co-ordinates two or more verbs with the same subject. All the verbs must have the same tense marker, which varies directly with the identity of the tense marker on the head verb. The abbreviation *tpe* stands for truncated personal ending, and appears in this construction when the head verb appears in the position specially designated for finite predicates; the abbreviation *te* stands for truncated ending, and occurs when the head verb appears in a construction that marks tense but not subject-verb agreement, e.g. the conditional, the adnominal participle. Further examples are found in (72).

TABLE 8: A Truncated SVF marking co-ordination between *vā-* 'come' and *suṛ-* 'see', Koṇḍa

	Singular		Plural	
1	*vā-t-a* come-pst-tpe 'I came and saw.'	*suṛ-t-a* see-pst-1s	*vā-t-a* come-pst-tpe 'We (not you) came and saw.'	*suṛ-t-ap* see-pst-1p^{ex}
			vā-t-a come-pst-tpe 'We (and you) came and saw.'	*suṛ-t-aṭ* see-pst-1p^{in}
2	*vā-t-i* come-pst-tpe 'You came and saw.'	*suṛ-t-i* see-pst-2s	*vā-t-i* come-pst-tpe 'You came and saw.'	*suṛ-t-ider* see-pst-2p
3m	*vā-t-a* come-pst-tpe 'He came and saw.'	*suṛ-t-an* see-pst-3sm	*vā-t-a* come-pst-tpe 'They came and saw.'	*suṛ-t-ar* see-pst-3pm
3n	*vā-t-a* come-pst-tpe 'It came and saw.'	*suṛ-t-ad* see-pst-3sn	*vā-t-e* come-pst-tpe 'Those things came and saw.'	*suṛ-t-e* see-pst-3pn

(72)(a) *vā-n-a* *sū-ṇ-a.*
come-npst-tpe see-npst-1s
'I will come and see.'

(b) *vā-n-a* *sū-ṇ-ap.*
come-npst-tpe see-npst-1pex
'We will come and see.'

(c) *so-n-a* *sū-ṇ-a* *vā-n-a* *ge.*
go-npst-tpe see-npst-tpe come-npst-1s indeed
'I'll go, see, and return.'

The Truncated SVFs in Table 8 encode the past tense marker, those in (72) the non-past tense marker. This kind of Truncated SVF in Koṇḍa functionally alternates with two fully finite verbs co-ordinated by the FPEC *-e* 'and, even'.

(73) (a) *vā-t-ider* *-e* *suṛ-t-ider.*
come-pst-2p and see-pst-2p
'You came and saw.'

(b) *vā-t-i* *suṛ-t-ider.*
come-pst-tpe see-pst-2p
'You came and saw.'

The two sentences in example (73) are semantically identical and probably co-derive from the same underlying structure. Full, repeated personal endings seem to occur only when there is a FPEC to support them, otherwise Affix-Truncation applies.

The examples in Table 8 and (72) do not fit our category of compound verbs. They most closely resemble those Dravidian constructions in which the conjunctive participle is used to co-ordinate several different verbs with the same subject, as illustrated in Chapter I. They are not FPE constructions, however, because they lack FPEs in surface structure.[3] These Truncated SVFs still conform to the definition of the SVF: they are constructions that consist of several component verbs which occur within a single RDFP or DDFP.

Koṇḍa also has examples of Truncated SVFs which are compound verbs. Most of them are auxiliary compound verbs, made with such auxiliary verbs as *son* 'go', *si* 'give', *ta* 'bring', *ṛis* 'leave', *pok* 'leave off', *o* 'take'. All of these auxiliaries appear as the head of Truncated SVFs.

(74) (a) *ek-t-a* *ṛis-t-a.*
climb-pst-tpe leave-pst-1s.
'I climbed up.'

(b) *tōṛis-n-a* *sī-n-a.*
show-npst-tpe give-npst-1s
'I will show (you).'

(c) *ribis-n-a* *ta-n-aṭ.*
release-npst-tpe bring- npst-1p^{in}
'We will get (them) released.'

(d) *si-t-a* *pok-t·an.*
give-pst-tpe leave off-pst-3sm
'He gave (it) away.'

(e) *tep-n-e* *o-n-e.*
pluck-npst-tpe take-npst-3sm
'They will pluck (it) off.'

(f) *sā-t-i* *so-R-iŋ . . .*
die-pst-te go-pst-cond
'If (they) had died . . .'

Most of these auxiliaries appear to signal the completion or culmination of an action. Although these auxiliary compound verbs differ from the co-ordinate structures above, their overall gross structure is that of a Truncated SVF.

Earlier mention has been made of a subset of Truncated SVFs which are exceptions to the condition that the tense markers of all the verbs within the SVF should be the same. This subset concerns Truncated SVFs that are built on the progressive/perfect auxiliary verb *man* 'be'. While the tense on the main verb is invariably past, the tense of the auxiliary may be past in which case it conveys the past progressive or pluperfect, or non-past, in which case it conveys present progressive or present perfect.

(75)(a) *veyu* *kāk-t-a* *ma-R-ar.*
mouth open-pst-tpe be-pst-3pm
'Their mouths were open/had opened.'

(b) *veyu* *kāk-t-a* *ma-n-ar.*
mouth open-pst-tpe be-npst-3pm
'Their mouths are open/have opened.'

(76)(a) *gūri-t-a* *ma-R-an.*
sleep-pst-tpe be-pst-3sm
'He was sleeping/had slept.'

(b) *gūri-t-a* *ma-n-an.*
sleep-pst-tpe be-npst-3sm
'He is sleeping/has slept.'

(77)(a) *vēnṛu* *iḍ-t-i* *ma-R-i* *gōsi* *uRpa-t-an.*
he-nom place-pst-te be-pst-adnp loincloth wear-pst-3sm
'He put on the loin cloth that that man had placed there.'

The pairs of examples in (75) and (76) are minimal pairs: the interpretation of the tense of these examples as past progressive/perfect or present progressive/perfect depends on whether the tense marker on the auxiliary verb *man* 'be' is past or nonpast. These Truncated SVFs certainly come from earlier, full SVFs: they are cognate with truncated forms in Pengo, and full SVFs in Parji.

The Past Negative in Koṇḍa

Examples from Tamil, Kannaḍa, Kota, Toda, Telugu, and Goṇḍi have shown that negation may be expressed by means of a SVF which uses the auxiliary verb **ā-* 'become' (*DEDR* 333), or its suppletive variants. Although the past negative conjugation in Koṇḍa is a synthetic verb form, it can be shown (Steever 1987) to descend from an earlier SVF that is cognate morpheme for morpheme with the past negative SVFs in Old Telugu and Muria Goṇḍi. The process of Affix-Truncation plays an important role in the fusion of the two parts of the auxiliary compound verb: the fusion is completed by the deletion of the lexical base of the auxiliary *ā-* 'become'. The bulk of the arguments for the history of this form are presented in Steever (1987). The past negative is illustrated in Table 9, its underlying source in Table 10.

TABLE 9 : The Koṇḍa Past Negative, *ta-/te-* 'bring'.

	Singular	Plural	
1	*te-ʔ-e*^{1}*-t-a*^{1}	*te-ʔ-e*^{1}*-t-aṭ*^{1}	(incl)
		te-ʔ-e^{1}*-t-ap*^{1}	(excl)
2	*te-ʔ-i*^{1}*-t-i*^{1}	*te-ʔ-i*^{1}*-t-ider*^{1}	
3m	*te-ʔ-e*^{1}*-t-an*^{1}	*te-ʔ-e*^{1}*-t-ar*^{1}	
3n	*te-ʔ-e*^{1}*-t-ad*^{1}	*te-ʔ-u*^{1}*-t-e*^{1}	

TABLE 10: The Reconstructed Koṇḍa Past Negative, *ta-/te-* 'bring',

	Singular	Plural	
1	* *te-ʔ-e##ā-t-a*	* *te-ʔ-eṭ##ā-t-aṭ*	(incl)
		* *te-ʔ-ep##ā-t-ap*	(excl)
2	* *te-ʔ-i##ā-t-i*	* *te-ʔ-ider##ā-t-ider*	
3m	* *te-ʔ-en##ā-t-an*	* *te-ʔ-er##ā-t-ar*	
3n	* *te-ʔ-ed##ā-t-ad*	* *te-ʔ-u##-ā-t-e*	

The forms in Table 9 have been segmented, and so contain a number of diacritics: the most striking of these is $X^1 \ldots X^1$, which signals a discontinuous personal ending, the remnants of two congruent personal endings. The personal endings of the past negative are in fact discontinuous morphs that are circumfixed around the tense marker. They evolved as the application of Affix-Truncation and the deletion of the auxiliary *ā-* 'become' eroded the boundary between the main and auxiliary verbs. This historical change is presented in Chart 1 as a generative phonological derivation. Four cells of the paradigm are included: the first person singular the first person plural inclusive, the second person plural, the third person plural neuter. Three rules apply in these derivations. The rule of AUXILIARY CONTRACTION (AC) applies to replace the word boundary between the main and auxiliary verbs with a simple morpheme boundary: this signals the initial contraction of two independent words, and feeds the subsequent rules. The next rule to apply is Affix-Truncation (AT) which replaces a personal ending with the form -$(((V_1)C_1)V_2C_2)$ by -V_1 in all but the last verb in the SVF. AUXILIARY VERB DELETION (AVD) deletes the lexical base of the auxiliary verb *ā-*'become', leaving behind only the tense marker and personal endings for which the auxiliary is inflected.[4] The output of these derivations is the paradigm in Table 9.

CHART 1: Sample Derivations of the Past Negative, *ta-/te-* 'bring', Koṇḍa

	1s	*/te-ʔ-e#ā-t-a/*	1p^in	*/te-ʔ-eṭ#ā-t-aṭ/*
AC		*te-ʔ-e-ā-t-a*		*te-ʔ-eṭ-ā-t-aṭ*
AT		*te-ʔ-e-ā-t-a*		*te-ʔ-e-ā-t-aṭ*
AVD		*te-ʔ-e-t-a*		*te-ʔ-e-t-aṭ*
	2p	*/te-ʔ-ider#ā-t-ider/*	3pn	*/te-ʔ-u#ā-t-e/*
AC		*te-ʔ-ider-ā-t-ider*		*te-ʔ-u-ā-t-e*
AT		*te-ʔ-i-ā-t-ider*		*te-ʔ-u-ā-t-e*
AVD		*te-ʔ-i-t-ider*		*te-ʔ-u-t-e*

The underlying form of the main verb of the SVF in Table 10 is the actual form of the simple, tenseless negative in Koṇḍa; the underlying form of the auxiliary, the actual form of the past conjugation of *ā-* 'become'. The rules of Auxiliary Contraction, Affix-Truncation, and Auxiliary Verb Deletion are independently motivated in the grammar of Koṇḍa, and elsewhere in South-Central Dravidian. The derivations in Chart 1 are straightforward, and on the strength of their Tamil and Goṇḍi cognates can be supposed to represent an actual historical change. The general trend from analysis to synthesis among the complex, exotic conjugations in South-Central Dravidian (Steever 1979, 1984, 1987) need not concern us here. What matters for our present purpose is that many of these contracted structures descend from earlier SVFs.

SUMMARY

The SVF in Konḍa appears in three stages of evolution: first, the balance SVFs represent a pristine stage of full-fledged SVFs; second, the Truncated SVFs represent a departure from the transparent structure of the first stage; and, third, the past negative conjugation contains the fossilized remains of an ancient SVF, whose only telltale is the presence of discontinuous personal endings. There is also a broad range of synchronic variation. While the majority of SVFs seem to be compound verbs of one kind or other, co-ordinate verb constructions are robustly represented. The compound verb may well stand at the core of constructions that can be SVFs, and other structures are admitted into the fold as they more nearly approximate the grammatical properties of compound verbs. Recall that the co-ordinate SVFs have to have the same tense marker and the same subject for each conjunct in the structure. In this way it resembles the restriction that associates just one set of grammatical features to the components of a compound verb. The Tamil data in (50) and (51), when compared with the Konḍa co-ordinate SVFs, appears to corroborate the relative antiquity of co-ordinate SVFs. Nevertheless, the set of Truncated SVFs in Konḍa has grown to include some constructions that do not technically fit our definition of the SVF. Affix-Truncation applies not just to SVFs but also to verbal constructions that mark tense, but not subject-verb agreement, e.g. the conditional in (74)f, the adnominal participle in (77). Determining the underlying source of these examples is a thorny problem. Does each verb in the structure underlying *sāti soRiŋ* 'if died' in (74)f have a conditional morpheme, or just the head verb? If, as seems likely, only the head verb marks the conditional morpheme, then the pattern of truncation in these examples is not morphological, but purely phonological. Indeed, the trend in modern Konḍa seems to be to reinterpret Affix-Truncation as a purely phonological pattern. Since, however, the cognates of the progressive/perfect tense series and the past negative conjugation are all SVFs, we may safely conclude that Truncated SVFs originated from ordinary SVFs.

4. PENGO

The four following examples from Burrow and Bhattacharya (1970) contain SVFs: the first three are balance compound verbs, the fourth a co-ordinate verb construction.

(78)(a) *biba* *injo* *ō-t-i* *samgiri*
marriage house-loc take-pst-adnp provisions
u-ṭ-ar *ti-c-ar* (2.47).
drink-pst-3pm eat-pst-3pm
'They consumed the provisions brought to the marriage house.'

(b) *narpur* *ebe* *ke* *rat-n-ah* *jut-n-ah*
world of men there indeed drop-npst-1p descend-npst-1p
de *i-c-ar* (1.102).
indeed say-pst-3pm
'They said, "We will take (it) down to the world of men".'

(c) *iver* *nar* *ubja-ta-r-na* *jarman*
these men man be born-pres prf-3pm birth
ā-ta-r-na (1.8).
become-pres prf-3pm
'These human being have been born.'

(d) *buga* *buga* *i-c-at,* *ūm-t-at* *rayla* *mato*
buga *buga* say-pst-3sn fly-pst-3sn *rayla* tree-loc
kuc-ka-t-at (12.66).
sit-go-pst-3sn
'It uttered the cry "buga buga," flew about, and settled on a Rayla tree.'

The balance SVF *uṭar ticar* 'they consumed' in (78)a consists of the two finite verb *uṭar* 'they drank' and *ticar* 'they ate'; and, aside from the difference in linear order, may be positively identified with the Koṇḍa balance SVF *tinad uṇad* 'it consumed' in (71)a. The balance SVF *nar ubjatarna jarman ātarna* 'they have been born' in (78)b resembles the Koṇḍa balance SVFs in (71)c-e in that each of the components is itself internally complex, consisting of a noun and finite verb form. Finally, example (78)d seems to contain a co-ordinate SVF, whose three conjuncts, *icat* 'it said', *ūmtat* 'it flew', and *kuckatat* 'it settled down', each mark the same tense and subject-verb agreement. In this it resembles the Koṇḍa co-ordinate SVFs in (74)f and (77), as well as the Tamil examples in (50).

The Present Perfect Tense Series

Analysis of the present perfect tense series in Pengo (Steever 1984) reveals that it descends from a SVF in much the same way that that past negative conjugation in Koṇḍa does. Since this etymology is presented and justified at length in Steever (1984), only a brief version need be given here. Mention should be made at the outset that the reconstructed form of the present perfect in Pengo corresponds morpheme for morpheme with both the paradigm that underlies the truncated present perfect series in Koṇḍa, e.g. (74), and the attested present perfect in Parji. This set of correspondences permits reconstruction of this particular SVF to the Proto-Dravidian era.

Examination of the present perfect series initially reveals a striking fact: it includes three formally distinct paradigms, each of which freely varies with the others. Neither syntactic, semantic, nor pragmatic differences have been found to distinguish the three. Burrow and Bhattacharya (1970) advance the proposal that each represents a different stage in a linear historical development while Steever (1984) argues that they are parallel developments that result from the differential application of Affix-Truncation to the repeated personal endings in the single SVF that underlies all three. The three different paradigms are presented in Tables 11, 12, and 13.

TABLE 11 : Present Perfect, Variant I, *huṛ-* 'see', Pengo

	Singular		Plural
1	*huṛ-t-aŋ-na*		*huṛ-t-ah-na* (excl)
			huṛ-t-ap-na (incl)
2	*huṛ-t-ay-na*		*huṛ-t-ader-na*
3m	*huṛ-t-an-na*	m	*huṛ-t-ar-na*
f, n	*huṛ-t-at-na*	f	*huṛ-t-ik-na*
		n	*huṛ-t-iŋ-na*

TABLE 12 : Present Perfect, Variant II, *huṛ-* 'see', Pengo

	Singular		Plural
1	*huṛ-t-aŋ-n-aŋ*		*huṛ-t-ah-n-as* (excl)
			huṛ-t-ap-n-ap (incl)
2	*huṛ-t-ay-n-ay*		——
3m	*huṛ-t-an-n-an*	m	*huṛ-t-ar-n-ar*
f, n	*huṛ-t-at-n-at*	f	*huṛ-t-ik-n-ik*
		n	*huṛ-t-iŋ-n-iŋ*

TABLE 13 : Present Perfect, Variant III, *huṛ-* 'see', Pengo

	Singular		Plural
1	*huṛ-tan-aŋ*		*huṛ-tan-as* (excl)
			huṛ-tan-ap (incl)
2	*huṛ-tan-ay*		*huṛ-tan-ider*
3m	*huṛ-tan-an*	m	*huṛ-tan-ar*
f, n	*huṛ-tan-at*	f	*huṛ-tin-ik*
		n	*huṛ-tin-iŋ*

Let us compare the three variants of the present perfect, taking the third person singular masculine as our standard of comparison. The forms *huṛ-t-an-na, huṛ-t-an-n-an,* and *huṛ-tan-an* all have the meaning 'he has seen'. The first variant, *huṛ-t-an-na,* consists of the verb base *huṛ* 'see', the present perfect tense marker *-t...na,* and the personal ending for the third person singular masculine *-an-*. Note that the tense marker is a discontinuous morph circumfixed around the personal ending. The second variant, *huṛ-t-an-n-an,* consists of the verb base *huṛ-* 'see', the present perfect tense marker *-t...n-*, and the personal ending of the third person singular masculine *-an ...an.* Observe that in this variant both the tense marker and the personal ending are discontinuous morphs, and that they are intercalated. The third variant *huṛ-tan-an* consists of the verb base *huṛ-* 'see', the present perfect tense marker *-tān-*, and the personal ending of the third person masculine singular *-an.* The allomorphy of the tense marker and the personal ending is perplexing, not in the least because some of the allomorphs are discontinuous, which is a rarity in Dravidian morphology. The allomorphs of a given morpheme are generally thought to occur in forms that are in complementary distribution, not ones in free variation. Finally, circumfixation is a very rare morphological process in Dravidian.

Steever (1984) proposes an etymology to solve these and related problems in the analysis of the present perfect in Pengo. It is argued that all three paradigms descend form a common proto-paradigm which is a SVF; that the same linguistic rules apply in their derivations; and that they differ only in the application of Affix-Truncation. The proto-paradigm appears in Table 14.

TABLE 14 : Reconstructed Present Perfect in Pengo, *huṛ-* 'see'

	Singular		Plural
1	* *huṛ-t-aŋ # man-n-aŋ*		* *huṛ-t-as # man-n-as* (excl)
			* *huṛ-t-ap # man-n-ap* (incl)
2	* *huṛ-t-ay # man-n-ay*		* *huṛ-t-ader # man-n-ader*
3m	* *huṛ-t-an # man-n-an*	m	* *huṛ-t-ar # man-n-ar*
f, n	* *huṛ-t-at # man-n-at*	f	* *huṛ-t-ik # man-n-ik*
		n	* *huṛ-t-iŋ # man-n-iŋ*

The reconstructed form of the third person singular masculine in Table 14 is the SVF **huṛ-t-an man-n-an* 'he has seen': the main verb **huṛtan* 'he saw' is inflected for the past tense and a personal ending while the auxiliary verb **man-n-an* 'he is' is inflected for the non-past tense and a congruent personal ending. Both components of the SVF still occur in modern Pengo in other contexts. This reconstructed form is to be favorably compared with the Konḍa form *gūrita manan* 'he has slept' in (76)b which derives from the underlying form /*gūri-t-an man-n-an*/. More cognates are introduced in the next chapter.

Two groups of rules, one central and one peripheral, apply in the derivations of the three paradigms in Tables 11, 12, and 13. The central rules include Auxiliary Contraction, Affix-Truncation, and Auxiliary Verb Deletion. The first two rules resemble their Koṇḍa counterparts in all important respects. Auxiliary Verb Deletion removes the lexical base of the auxiliary verb *man* 'be', leaving behind the suffixes. While obligatory in Pengo, this last rule is still optional in Kūi, Kūvi, and the Alidibad dialect of Goṇḍi where complex tense forms permit the optional deletion of the auxiliary *man* 'be'. The peripheral rules include Nasal Degemination (ND) and Vowel Dissimilation (VD). The former applies before Auxiliary Contraction to replace two adjacent nasals in the auxiliary verb with one. Vowel Dissimilation changes a word-final *-i* into *-a* in the derivations of the third person plural feminine and neuter forms, representing an analogic restructuring so that all members of the paradigm end in *-na*. Chart 2 presents the derivation of four cells of the paradigm in Table 13: the first person singular, the second person plural, the third person singular masculine, and the third person plural feminine.

CHART 2: Sample Derivations of the Present Perfect, Variant III, Pengo.

	1s	/*huṛ-t-aŋ # man-n-aŋ*/	2p	/*huṛ-t-ader # man-n-ader*/
ND		*huṛ-t-aŋ # ma-n-aŋ*		*huṛ-t-ader # ma-n-ader*
AC		*huṛ-t-aŋ-ma-n-aŋ*		*hur-t-ader-ma-n-ader*
AT		*huṛ-t-a-ma-n-aŋ*		*huṛ-t-a-ma-n-ader*
AVD		*huṛ-t-a-n-aŋ*		*huṛ-t-a-n-ader*
	3sm	/*huṛ-t-an # man-n-an*/	3pf	/*huṛ-t-ik # man-n-ik*/
ND		*huṛ-t-an # ma-n-an*		*huṛ-t-ik # ma-n-ik*
AC		*huṛ-t-an-ma-n-an*		*huṛ-t-ik-ma-n-ik*
AT		*huṛ-t-a-ma-n-an*		*huṛ-t-i-ma-n-ik*
AVD		*huṛ-t-a-n-an*		*huṛ-t-i-n-ik*

Affix-Truncation applies in the derivation of the four cells in Chart 2 to shorten the personal ending of the main verb, whittling it down to its initial vowel. At this stage of the derivation, before the application of Auxiliary Verb Deletion, the intermediate derivational stage of the Pengo forms corresponds exactly to the attested Koṇḍa forms in (75) b and (76)b. The output of the derivations in Chart 2 is not strictly identical to the attested forms in Table 13: it must undergo another process to remove now extraneous morpheme boundaries so that *huṛ-t-a-n-an* is transformed into *huṛ-tan-an* 'he has seen', which is the properly segmented form in the modern language. Thus, the present perfect allomorph *-tan-* /*-tin-* results from the amalgamation of the *-t-* from the past tense marker, the *-a-* /*-i-* from a truncated personal ending, and the *-n-* from the non-past tense morpheme.

Chart 3 presents the derivation of four cells of the paradigm in Table 11. It proceeds in much the same way as the derivation in Chart 2, but with two differences. Affix-Truncation applies to the personal ending on the auxiliary, not the main verb. If the teleology of this rule is to reduce the redundancy of two identical personal endings in a SVF, then it can be satisfied by applying to either one. The grammar of Pengo permits such latitude in the application of Affix-Truncation. Next, the rule of Vowel Dissimilation applies to change the word-final *-ni* into *-na* in the third person plural feminine and neuter forms.

CHART 3 : Sample Derivations of the Present Perfect, Variant I, Pengo.

	1s	/*huṛ-t-aŋ # man-n-aŋ*/	2p	/*huṛ-t-ader # man-n-ader*/
ND		*huṛ-t-aŋ # ma-n-aŋ*		*huṛ-t-ader # ma-n-ader*
AC		*huṛ-t-aŋ-ma-n-aŋ*		*huṛ-t-ader-ma-n-ader*
AT		*huṛ-t-aŋ-ma-n-a*		*huṛ-t-ader-ma-n-a*
AVD		*huṛ-t-aŋ-n-a*		*huṛ-t-ader-n-a*
	3sm	/*huṛ-t-an # man-n-an*/	3pf	/*huṛ-t-ik # man-n-ik*/
ND		*huṛ-t-an # ma-n-an*		*huṛ-t-ik # ma-n-ik*
AC		*huṛ-t-an-ma-n-an*		*huṛ-t-ik-ma-n-ik*
AT		*huṛ-t-an-ma-n-a*		*huṛ-t-ik-ma-n-i*
AVD		*huṛ-t-an-n-a*		*huṛ-t-ik-n-i*
VD		. . . dna . . .		*huṛ-t-ik-n-a*

The output of the derivations in Chart 3 is not identical with the attested forms collated in Table 11 because their segmentations differ. Additional morphological processes must apply to remove the boundary that immediately precedes the word-final *-a,* so that *huṛ-t-an-n-a* is re-analyzed as *huṛ-t-an–na* 'he has seen'. The restructuring of this form, represented by the new segmentation, takes place under the impact of general morphological processes that eliminate non-functional morpheme boundaries, not by some rule that is peculiar to this derivation. The present perfect allomorph *-t ... na* is the historical amalgam of the *-t-* of the past tense marker, the *-n-* of the non-past tense marker, and the *-a-* of the truncated personal endings—some by way of *-i*. It owes its discontinuity to the fact that the tense markers originally occurred in two separate verb forms in the SVF.

Chart 4 presents the derivation of the present perfect in Table 12. It is once again the differential application of Affix-Truncation that is responsible for differentiating this paradigm from the other two. In this instance Affix-Truncation fails to apply, and the immediate result is a set of discontinuous personal endings. However, the second person plural is a positive absolute exception to Affix-Truncation, and must therefore undergo some form of the rule: in Chart 4 the personal ending on the main verb is truncated, yielding the corresponding form of Variant III, although it could as easily have been the one of the auxiliary, yielding the corresponding form of Variant I.

CHART 4 : Sample Derivations of the Present Perfect, Variant II, Pengo.

	1s	*/huṛ-t-aŋ # man-n-aŋ/*	2p	*/huṛ-t-ader # man-n-ader/*
ND		*huṛ-t-aŋ # ma-n-aŋ*		*huṛ-t-ader # ma-n-ader*
AC		*huṛ-t-aŋ-ma-n-aŋ*		*huṛ-t-ader-ma-n-ader*
AT		. . . dna . . .		*huṛ-t-a-ma-n-ader*
AVD		*huṛ-t-aŋ-n-aŋ*		*huṛ-t-a-n-ader*
	3sm	*/huṛ-t-an # man-n-an/*	3pf	*/huṛ-t-ik # man-n-ik/*
ND		*huṛ-t-an # ma-n-an*		*huṛ-t-ik # ma-n-ik*
AC		*huṛ-t-an-ma-n-an*		*huṛ-t-ik-ma-n-ik*
AT		. . . dna . . .		. . . dna . . .
AVD		*huṛ-t-an-n-an*		*huṛ-t-ik-n-ik*

None of the present perfect forms with discontinuous personal endings needs to undergo further morphological resegmentation: the synchronic morphology must assure only that the *-t-* and *-n-* are interpreted as a discontinuous allomorph of the present perfect, and that the repeated personal endings are also interpreted as a discontinuous allomorph of the personal endings. Affix-Truncation does not apply (dna) in the derivations in Chart 4 except in the second person plural.

Thus, the rule of Affix-Truncation is optional. It need not apply, and if it does not, the forms in Table 12 result. But if it does apply, then it may apply to the personal ending on the main verb or the auxiliary verb. In the first instance, the forms in Table 13 are generated; in the second, the forms in Table 11. It is thus the optional and largely unconditioned application of Affix-Truncation that gives rise to the three different allo-paradigms of the present perfect, and to the use of discontinuous morphs. All three variants descend from a single proto-paradigm, one which is a SVF.

The Synthetic Present Perfect in Tamil

The analysis of the present perfect tense series in Pengo provides us with the raw material and the tools to identify a cognate in Tamil: the synthetic present perfect. It is usually said that Classical Tamil verbs may have two past tense forms, one simple and the other complex. In the simple form, which is the most familiar, the past tense marker and the personal ending join together without any intervening material, e.g. *kaṇ-ṭ-ēṉ* 'I saw'. In the complex form, on the other hand, the past tense marker and personal ending are separated by the formative *-aṉ-*, e.g. *kaṇ-ṭ-aṉ-eṉ* 'I saw'.[5] I believe that this so-called past tense form is really a remnant of the Proto-Dravidian perfect tense series with the auxiliary verb **man* 'be' (*DEDR* 4778), and is therefore cognate with the present perfect forms in Koṇḍa, Pengo, and Parji. The so-called past tense marker *-(n)taṉ-* is really the present perfect tense marker. This form is henceforth called the synthetic present perfect. It flourished in Classical Tamil, and was lost in all the modern dialects except Sri Lankan Tamil. The examples from the classical language in (79) and from Sri Lankan Tamil in (80) are best interpreted as markers of the present perfect, not the past tense.

(79) (a) *kuṉṟum malaiyum pala piṉ oẓiya va-ntaṉ-eṉ*
hill-and mountian-and many behind pass-inf come-pres prf-1s
paricil koṇ-ṭaṉ-eṉ celaṟku (*puṟanāṉūṟu* 208.1-2).
gifts bring-pres prf-1s spread-vn-dat
'I have come across many hills and mountains; I have brought gifts to distribute.'

(b) *aṟaṉ il āḷaṉōṭu iṟa-ntaṉ-aḷ iṉi maṟantu*
virtue not man-soc go-pres prf-3sf still forget-cp
amaintu irāa neñcam nōvēṉ (*akanāṉūṟu* 219.10).
be still-cp be-neg-adnp heart ache-neg-1s
'Even though she has gone away with a virtueless man, I will not grieve with a restless, unforgetting heart.'

(c) *kaṇ-ṭaṉ-aṉ kaṟpiṉukku ayiṇaik kaṅkaḷāl teṇṭirai*
see-pres prf-1s fidelity-dat jewel eye-p-instr cool wave
yalaikaṭal ilaṅkait teṉṉakar (*kāmpa rāmāyaṇam* 1308.1).
billow sea Lanka south city
'I have seen her, the jewel of fidelity, with my own eyes, in the South City of Lanka, washed by the cool waves of the billowing seas.'

(80) (a) *atukkut tāṉ nāṉ appaṭic coṉ-ṉaṉ-āṉ.*
that-dat indeed I-nom that way say-pres prf-1s
'That's why I have said so.'

(b) *nī* *kaṭaṉ* *vāṅki* *araikkotta* *ariciyaiyum*
you-nom loan take-cp grind-pst-adnp rice-acc-and
vāṅkuvam *eṇṭu* *tāṉ* *va-ntaṉ-āṉ*.
take-hrt say-cp indeed come-pres prf-1s
'I have come to get the ground rice you borrowed.'

(c) *ippa* *tāṉ* *kaṭaikku* *va-ntaṉ-ī-(y)ē*.
now indeed store-dat come-pres prf-2s-emp
'So you have just now come to the store.'

(d) *ivvaḷavu* *nēram* *eṉṉa* *mīṉ* *piṭic-caṉ-īṅkaḷ-ē*.
this much time what fish catch-pres prf-2p-emp
'You have caught so many fish in this (short) time!'

Although Gair and Suseendirarajah (1981) believe that the forms in Sri Lankan Tamil are innovations within that dialect, phonological and morphological comparison with the forms in Classical Tamil strongly suggests that they are retentions of the synthetic present perfect. The only difference is in the allomorphy of the personal endings: while the personal endings in Classical Tamil have short vowels, those in Sri Lankan Tamil have long vowels. This can be explained as a side-effect of the historical changes that have progressively reduced the allomorphic variation among the personal endings in favor of those forms with long vowels.

The derivation of the synthetic present perfect form is illustrated in Chart 5 with one verb from Classical Tamil, *vantaṉeṉ* 'I have come', and one from Sri Lankan Tamil, *piṭiccaṉīṅkaḷ* 'you have caught'. This derivation uses essentially the same rules that figured in the derivation of the present perfect in Pengo. Some variation is present in the exact formulation of these rules, however. Affix-Truncation in Tamil removes the entire personal ending, leaving behind no telltale vowel as in Pengo and Koṇḍa. In this respect, Affix-Truncation is the reverse of Rule (45), and is independently needed in Tamil to describe the alternation between the full SVFs in (46) and their plain compound verb counterparts in (48). Auxiliary verb Deletion does not excise the entire lexical base of the auxiliary verb *maṉ* 'be', but just its initial consonant *m*.[6] Such a rule is independently required in Classical Tamil for the derivation of the form *eṉm-aṉār* 'they (will) say' from *eṉṉum maṉār* 'they (will) say' (see Steever 1984: 640). Finally, the phonological rule of Palatalization (P) operates in the modern language to convert a dental consonant cluster following a front high vowel into a palatal. As in Pengo, principles of morphology will restructure the output of Chart 5 to remove extraneous morpheme boundaries so that *va-nt-a-ṉ-eṉ* becomes the properly segmented form *va-ntaṉ-eṉ* 'I have come'.

CHART 5: The Derivation of the Synthetic Present Perfect in Tamil.

	1p		2p
	/va-nt-en̲ # man̲-n̲-en̲/		*/piṭi-tt-iṅkaḷ # man̲-n̲-iṅkaḷ/*
ND	*va-nt-en̲ # ma-n̲-en̲*		*piṭi-tt-iṅkaḷ # ma-n̲-iṅkaḷ*
P	. . . dna . . .		*piṭi-cc-iṅkaḷ # ma-n̲-iṅkaḷ*
AC	*va-nt-en-ma-n̲-en̲*		*piṭi-cc-iṅkaḷ-ma-n̲-iṅkaḷ*
AT	*va-nt-ma-n̲-en̲*		*piṭi-cc-ma-n̲-iṅkaḷ*
AVD	*va-nt-a-n̲-en̲*		*piṭi-cc-a-n̲-iṅkaḷ*

The derivations in Chart 5 proceed straightforwardly, and yield the forms of the synthetic present perfect in Tamil. Over the past 1000 years these forms have retreated before the analytic auxiliary compound verb with *irukka* 'be' (Steever 1983: 308, pass.). That they persist in Sri Lankan Tamil is an immense boon to those who wish to study the history ofthis form and its interpretation. But such a study clearly goes beyond the dimensions of this book. What matters here is that the Tamil evidence helps to confirm the presence of a SVF that encodes the perfect tense at any early stage of Dravidian.

5. KŪVI

Kūvi has iterative and echo compound verbs which are SVFs: both are lexical compound verbs in which both the tense marker and the personal ending agree from one verb to the next in the SVF. Consider the following examples.

(81)(a) *jāp-mu* *gīp-mu.*
teach-imp(2p) *gi*-imp(2p)
'Teach us or do something like that.'

(b) *embaṭiʔe* *buṛhi-buṛha* *ma-c-eri* *ma-c-eri* *iṅjaha*
there old woman-old man be-pst-3pm be-pst-3pm say-cp
hāha *ha-c-eri.*
die-cp go-pst-3pm
'The old man and woman lived on and on there, and died.'

(c) *kokari* *pari-t-eri* *pari-t-eri* *inja* *nāṭa*
boys search-pst-3pm search-pst-3pm say-cp village-loc
veska *ha-c-eri.*
tell-inf go-pst-3pm
'The boys searched and searched, and went to the village to report.'

(d) *ḍōriti* *himborita* *poji-t-esi,* *ṭenga* *ḍēki-t-esi* *va-t-esi,*
rope cloth-soc cover-pst-3sm stick carry-pst-3sm come-pst-3sm

injaha *buṛhini* *ele* *i-c-esi.*
say-cp wife-acc thus say-pst-3sm
'He covered the rope with his cloth, brought the stick, and spoke thus to his wife.'

The *gi*-echo compound verb *jāpmu gīpmu* 'teach' (us) or do something like that' in (81)a is based on the imperative *jāpmu* 'teach', a finite form. The iterative compound verbs *maceri maceri* 'they lived on and on' in (81)b and *pariteri pariteri* 'they searched and searched' in (81)c are based on the finite verbs *maceri* 'they were' and *pariteri* 'they searched', respectively. Both varieties of the SVF has been studied already, e.g. in Kannaḍa. The conjunctive participles *inja* and *injaha* in (81) b-d derive from the FPEP **en* 'say, think', but have many of the properties of co-ordinating conjunctions in modern Kūvi. That noted, we may extract the SVF *ḍēkitesi vatesi* 'he brought' from the second conjunct of the co-ordinate structure in (81)c. This SVF is a descriptive lexical compound verb consisting of the two finite verbs *ḍēkitesi* 'he carried' and *vatesi* 'he came'. This SVF belongs to the same class of lexical compound verbs as the more familiar Tamil compound verb *koṇṭu vara* 'to bring', a plain compound verb that consists of the conjunctive participle of *koḷḷa* 'hold' and an inflected form of *vara* 'come'. Here, however, each component of the compound verb is formally finite. Although Kūvi lacks the array of auxiliary compound verbs that many of its sister languages have, it displays a full range of lexical compound verbs which are SVFs. As we continue to see more and more Kūvi material reach print, we shall doubtlessly discover more SVFs.

6. SUMMARY

The SVF is quite well represented in the South-Central Dravidian subgroup. Auxiliary compound verbs for the past negative, and the present perfect are extensively dispersed throughout the group; balance, iterative, and echo compound verbs are easily found; and co-ordinate verb constructions are present, as well.

Chapter Five

SERIAL VERBS IN CENTRAL DRAVIDIAN

1. INTRODUCTION

Parji, Kolami, and Ollari (also known as Koṇekor Gadaba) have several varieties of SVF, all of which have already been observed to occur in the south and south-central subgroups. The published material on the languages of the Central Dravidian subgroup is scanty, so the survey of this branch is necessarily brief. Nevertheless, several specific SVFs are shown to be the exact cognates of SVFs in other languages, allowing us to project them to an early stage of common Dravidian. Their evidence helps us to confirm the essentially Dravidian origin and nature of the SVF.

2. PARJI

A cursory search of Burrow and Bhattacharya's (1953) texts reveals the two following SVFs, one a co-ordinate verb construction and the other a balance compound verb. Though they occur infrequently, there can be little doubt that they are easily integrated into the grammar of Parji.

(82) (a) *baṛal-in* *en-mote-d* *caruk-mote-d.*
bullock-acc speak-pres-3sm drive-pres-3sm
'He drove the bullocks (by) speaking to them.'

(b) *pāv* *patti* *cen-d-ar* *ōṛ* *patti* *cen-d-ar.*
path take-cp go-pst-3pm path take-cp go-pst-3pm
'They went by the path.'

The SVF *enmoted carukmoted* 'he drove by speaking' in (82)a is a co-ordinate verb construction, and resembles the Tamil SVFs in (50), the Konḍa examples in (74)f and (77), and the Pengo example in (78)d. The balance SVF in (82) consists of two parts, each of which has a noun followed by the postposition *patti* 'by means of' and the finite verb form *cendar* 'they went'. This example implies the existence of the balance noun *pāv-ōṛ* 'path', which is split into its component parts in the balance SVF. This construction is to be compared with Konḍa balance SVFs in (71)c-e and the Pengo example (78)c. Thus, both kinds of SVF independently occur in the south-central subgroup.

The Present Perfect Tense Series

Burrow and Bhattacharya (1953: 58) describe a compound verb that is "...a combination of the past tense form of the verb with the present (future in form) of the verb 'to be'." Both verbs are formally finite, having tense markers and congruent personal endings. This compound is therefore a SVF, and conveys the meaning of the present progressive or, according to context, the present perfect. It is in every respect an exact cognate of the reconstructed present perfect forms in Pengo, as illustrated in Table 14. Unlike Pengo and Konḍa, however, Parji has preserved this SVF in its pristine, uncontracted form.

(83) (a) *un-d-ed* *mĕ-d-ad.*
sit-pst-3sm be-npst-3sm
'He is sitting/has sat.'

(b) *nil-t-en* *mĕ-d-an.*
stand-pst-1s be-npst-1s
'I am standing.'

(c) *pāp* *cā-j-en* *mĕ-d-an.*
evil do-pst-1s be-npst-1s
'I have done evil.'

(d) *ām* *pan-ḍ-om* *mĕ-d-am.*
we-nom tire-pst-1p be-npst-1p
'We are tired.'

(e) *ḍū* *meramti* *paka-t-o* *mĕ-d-a.*
tiger-nom jungle-loc lurk-pst-3n be-npst-3n
'The tiger is lurking in the jungle.'

(f) *īn* *pat-t-ot* *mĕ-d-at.*
you-nom hold-pst-2s be-npst-2s
'You are holding him.'

(g) *enot* *cāva* *end-r-ed* *mĕ-d-ad*?
how much gruel bring-pst-3sm be-npst-3sm
'How much gruel has he brought?'

As in Konḍa and Pengo, the interpretation of these Parji forms is present progressive or present perfect, depending as the aspectual class of the main verb is imperfective or perfective. Even though the past and non-past tenses of Parji have separate allomorphs of the personal endings, the categories they morphologically encode are the same. Comparison of these forms with those in Konḍa and Pengo reveals a point-by-point, morpheme-by-morpheme correspondence. Burrow and Bhattacharya remark that this compound verb is very common in Parji, a statement which can be verified by reading the texts.

Parji also has plain compound verbs that are constructed with the non-finite bare verb base (Burrow and Bhattacharya 1953: 44, pass.). As noted above, such a construction often occurs in the same language as a SVF, and represents the kind of structure that is the input to Rule (45). Corresponding to the structural change of Rule (45) are subject-predicate agreement rules, which in Parji apply to predicate nominals (Burrow and Bhattacharya 1953: 26) and predicate adjectives (*ibid*, 32).

3. KOLAMI

Emeneau's (1955: 101) grammar of Kolami records two variants of the *gi*-echo compound which alternate with each other. In the first variant, only the bare verb base is echoed; but in the second, the entire finite verb form is.

(84)(a) *aras-nem.*
fear-neg-imp
'Don't be afraid.'

(b) *araz-giras-nem.*
fear-*gi*-neg-imp.
'Don't be afraid or anything.'

(c) *aras-nem* *giras-nem.*
fear-neg-imp *gi*-neg-imp
'Don't be afraid or anything.'

Both the *gi*-echo compound verbs in (84)b and c are based on the simple prohibative, or negative imperative *arasnem* 'don't be afraid' in (84)a. Note that the variant in (84)b, which echoes only the bare verb base, corresponds to the Toda *ki*-echo compound verbs in (56); while the variant in (84)c corresponds to the Tamil example in (53)b and the Kannaḍa examples in (60). The former is a plain compound verb, the latter a SVF. What is important for our purposes is the fact that these two variants freely alternate within a single language, as well as across languages. Example (84)c is the only instance of a SVF in Kolami.

The Past Negative

Despite thorough restructuring, the Kolami past negative paradigm appears to have descended from an earlier SVF which is cognate with the attested forms in Old Telugu and Muria Gonḍi. First consider three finite paradigms of the verb *sī*- 'give' (*DEDR* 2598); the past affirmative in Table 15, the tenseless negative in Table 16, and the past negative in Table 17.

TABLE 15 : The Past Affirmative in Kolami, *sī-* 'give'

	Singular	Plural
1	*sī-t-an*	*sī-t-am*
2	*sī-t-iv*	*sī-t-ir*
3m	*sī-t-en*	*sī-t-er*
3n	*sī-t-ev*	*sī-t-in*

TABLE 16 : The Negative in Kolami, *sī-* 'give'

	Singular	Plural
1	*sī-en*	*sī-em*
2	*sī-ev*	*sī-er*
3m	*sī-en*	*sī-er*
3n	not attested	*sī-ed*

TABLE 17 : The Past Negative in Kolami, *sī-* 'give'

	Singular	Plural
1	*sī-e-t-an*	*sī-e-t-am*
2	*sī-e-t-iv*	*sī-e-t-ir*
3m	*sī-e-t-en*	*sī-e-t-er*
3n	*sī-e-t-ev*	*sī-e-t-in*

Note that the negative paradigm in Kolami has a special set of personal ending, e.g., *-en*, *-ev*, etc., which differs from the set used in the past affirmative, e.g., *-an*, *-iv*, etc. While the segmentation of the paradigm in Table 15 is Emeneau's, that in Tables 16 and 17 is mine. Emeneau analyzes the form *sīen* 'I do/will not give' into the base *sī-* 'give', the negative marker *-e-*, and the personal ending *-n* for the first person singular. Similarly, he analyzes the corresponding past negative form *sīetan* 'I did not give' into the base *sī-* 'give', the negative marker *-e-*, the past tense marker *-t-*, and the personal ending *-an*. There can be no doubt that the proper synchronic analysis of these two paradigms leads directly to Emeneau's segmentations. But comparison with the negative conjugation in other Dravidian languages suggests that the synchronic analysis represents a restructuring in the Kolami finite negative verbs. The segmentation of the negative forms which I give in Table 16 accords exactly with the segmentations of the cognate negative paradigm in Classical Tamil where *kāṇēṉ* 'I do/will not see' consists of the verb base *kāṇ-* 'see', a zero morph of the negative marker whose presence is reflected in the phonology of the preceding verb base, and the personal ending *-ēṉ* of the first person singular. If we accept the parallel treatment for pre-Kolami and associate the vowel *-e-* with the personal endings, then the past negative, as segmented in Table 17, matches the Koṇḍa past negative, as segmented in Table 9. This leads us to the provisional conclusion that in pre-Kolami, before a re-analysis shifted the morpheme boundary to create the *-e-* allomorph of the negative morpheme, the negative morpheme was instantiated by a zero allomorph in both the negative and the past negative paradigms. If, pursuing this line of argument, the Kolami past negative is derived in the same way as the Koṇḍa past negative, it must also come from an old SVF that consists of the tenseless negative of the main verb and the past affirmative of the auxiliary verb **ā-* 'become'.

This tentative derivation is illustrated in Chart 6, according to which the

CHART 6 : Derivation of the Past Negative in Kolami, *sī-* 'give'

	1s		2p	
		/sī-en ǂǂ ā-t-an/		*/sī-er ǂǂ ā-t-ir/*
AC		*sī-en-ā-t-an*		*sī-er-ā-t-ir*
AT		*sī-e-a-t-an*		*sī-e-a-t-ir*
AVD		*sī-e-t-an*		*sī-e-t-ir*

derivation of the Kolami past negative runs parallel to that of the Koṇḍa past negative in Chart 1. The primary difference between the two is the levelling of the vowel of the personal ending on the main verb so that all cells of the paradigm have *-e-* between the verb base and the past tense marker. The rules of Auxiliary Contraction, Affix-Truncation, and Auxiliary Verb Deletion apply here as before. Kolami shows traces of Affix-Truncation and Auxiliary Verb Deletion, as it pertains to **ā-* 'become', elsewhere in the grammar. Auxiliary Verb Deletion is responsible for the development of the FPECs *-te* 'if' and *-tiri* 'even if' from the FPEPs **ā-te* 'if becomes' and **ā-tiri* 'even if becomes', respectively (Steever 1987). Furthermore, Emeneau (1955: 18-9) observes that the personal ending of the first person singular future verb, *-un*, may optionally be deleted before the suffixes *-te* 'if' and *-tiri* 'even if', that is to say, in an environment that immediately precedes the slot where **ā-* 'become' is reconstructed. Thus, at least in one independent instance, a personal ending and the lexical base of the verb **ā-* 'become' are removed.

Although the derivation of the Kolami past negative in Chart 6 appears to take a "free-ride" on rules that were established on the basis of alternations in other languages, historical considerations support their use in Kolami. The principles of comparative reconstruction should not lead to the postulation of two or more morphemically distinct, semantically equivalent, and freely varying past tense paradigms. We may expect to reconstruct only one past tense paradigm, with possibly several allomorphic variants. We are confronted here with two candidates for the reconstructed past negative paradigm: one is an analytic SVF, the other a synthetic simple verb. Since it is improbable that both can be reconstructed to the proto-language, one must be chosen. The distribution of past negative forms throughout the Dravidian family indicates that the past negative SVF, as found in Old Telugu and Muria Goṇḍi, is original, while the past negative synthetic forms, as found in Koṇḍa and Kolami, are innovations. Moreover, while we can explain the development of synthetic simple verbs from analytic compound verbs with the process of Auxiliary Contraction, we cannot explain the reverse development except in the most *ad hoc* manner. Simple verb forms are not easily and systematically re-analyzed into a compound verb construction. The development of the Koṇḍa past negative corroborates this technical consideration. Three stages in the evolution of the past negative conjugation are present in this data: the original SVF in Old Telugu; the truncated, contracted SVF in Koṇḍa; and the highly levelled synthetic verb in Kolami. It may well be that the past negative paradigms in other languages, such as Kūi and Kūvi, belong to this third stage of evolution. Thus, if the Kolami past negative paradigm is cognate with the past negative conjugations in other Dravidian languages, it must descend from an earlier negative SVF.

4. OLLARI

P. S. Subrahmanyam (1971: 372) observes that the dialect of Ollari which S. Bhattacharya (1956) described possesses two SVFs. Both of them are auxiliary compound verbs that signal negation, and structurally resemble the negative conjugations we have already seen. In the texts of a closely related dialect, called Koṇekor Gadaba and studied by P. Bhaskararao (1980), examples may be found of balance SVFs.

In Ollari the past progressive negative is conveyed by a compound verb that consists of the non-past negative of the main verb and the past affirmative of the progressive auxiliary verb *man* 'be', with both inflected for congruent personal endings. Though the two components are separated by the so-called union vowel *-i-*, they nevertheless constitute a genuine SVF. This paradigm, presented in Table 18, appears to blend the features of the Pengo present perfect and the Koṇḍa past negative in one form by expressing the progressive tense of the former and the negation of the latter. Moreover, the auxiliary verb *man* 'be' appears where on comparative grounds we might expect some form of *ā- 'become' to occur. However, the auxiliary verb ā- 'become' appears to have lapsed from Ollari, certainly from the negative conjugation.

The form *īl-an-i ma-ṭ-on* 'I was not falling' consists of the tenseless negative of the main verb *īl-an* 'I did/do/will not fall', the union vowel *-i-*, and the past affirmative of the auxiliary verb *ma-ṭ-on* 'I was'. Since both auxiliary and main verb are formally finite, and have congruent personal endings, the whole compound is a SVF.

TABLE 18: The Past Progressive Negative in Ollari, *īl-* 'fall'

	Singular	Plural
1	*īl-an-i ma-ṭ-on*	*īl-am-i ma-ṭ-om*
2	*īl-at-i ma-ṭ-ot*	*īl-ar-i ma-ṭ-or*
3m	*īl-anḍ-i ma-ṭ-onḍ*	*īl-ar-i ma-ṭ-or*
3n	*īl-ad-i ma-ṭ-a*	*īl-av-i ma-ṭ-ev*

TABLE 19: The Present Progressive Negative in Ollari, *īl* 'fall'

	Singular	Plural
1	*īl-an-i ma-y-an*	*īl-am-i ma-y-am*
2	*īl-at-i ma-y-aṭ*	*īl-ar-i ma-y-ar*
3m	*īl-anḍ-i ma-y-anḍ*	*īl-ar-i ma-y-ar*
3n	*īl-ad-i ma-y-a*	*īl-av-i ma-y-av*

Table 19 displays the paradigm of the present progressive negative. It resembles the past progressive negative in every respect but one: the present tense marker *-y-* replaces the past tense marker *-ṭ-*. Consequently, a different set of allomorphs of the personal endings is selected. Whether or not these two paradigms can be projected to an early stage of common Dravidian, the process of generating SVFs for the negative conjugation certainly can be.

The two following SVFs come from Bhaskararao's (1980) texts, 1.75 and 2.35, respectively. Both appear to be balance compound SVFs.

(85) (a) *mūden* *sūḍi* *nette* *veḍ-d-a* *udlāku-d-a.*
rabbit-acc see-cp dog-nom run-pres-3sn chase-pres-3sn
'Seeing the rabbit, the dog chases after it.'

(b) *erik-k-av* *umbul-k-av* *inji* *ukuṭ-pel-i*
defecate-npst-3pn urinate-npst-3pn say-cp one-place-emp

ōḍi	*maŋgoṭ*	*sattuv*	*keyad*	*inji*
remain-cp	be-cond	strength	make-neg-3sn	say-cp
siṇḍupeṭi	*sāy-d-ar.*			
drive-cp	be-fut-3pm			

'They drive (the goats) so they excrete, because if the stay in one place, they do not fertilize (the whole land).'

The SVF *veḍda udlākuda* 'it chases after' in (85)a consists of the two finite verbs *veḍda* 'it runs' and *udlākuda* 'it chases', similarly, the SVF *erikkav umbulkav* 'they excrete' in (85) b consists of the two finite verbs *erikkav* 'they defecate' and *umbulkav* 'they urinate'. As is now to be expected the two components of each SVF have the same personal endings. Although Bhaskararao (1980) notes the presence of *gi*-echo formation in Koṇekor Gadaba, none of his examples contain SVFs. Since they exist both in Kolami and the geographically close Telugu, echo SVFs may well turn up as further research on Koṇekor Gadaba proceeds.

Chapter Six

SERIAL VERBS IN NORTH DRAVIDIAN

1. INTRODUCTION

THE three North Dravidian languages Kuṛux, Malto, and Brahui all have SVFs. Indeed, the SVF is so common in this subgroup that Emeneau (1980) considered it a shared innovation that distinguishes it from the rest of Dravidian. In view of the evidence adduced above, this hypothesis can no longer be maintained: the SVF belongs to the common Dravidian heritage. Even though linguists have lost the SVF as a means of defining the North Dravidian subgroup, they retain it as a way to include these three languages in the rest of the family.

Chapter II suggests that Rule (44) is not in its present form wholly applicable to the North Dravidian languages. Since the distribution of finite predicates is broader in this subgroup, it becomes somewhat harder to identify SVFs, particularly those that instantiate co-ordinate verb constructions. But even though these languages have relaxed the constraints on multiple finite predicates, one can still recognize in them structures that correspond to the RDFP and DDFP in the three other subgroups. These structures can have only one finite predicate, they may therefore potentially host the SVF. Comparison with the three other subgroups shows us that North Dravidian possesses SVFs that reflect the common Dravidian heritage, and support their reconstruction to the proto-language.

2. KUṚUX

The major grammars of Kuṛux, also known as Dhangar in Nepal, draw attention both to SVFs and to constructions that resemble them. Consider first of all the following examples from Hahn (1911).

(86) (a) *ēn* *ra'-ck-an* *bē'e-d-en.*
I-nom be-pst-1s be-pres-1s
'I have remained there.'

(b) *nīn* *ra'-ck-ai* *bē'e-d-ai.*
you-nom be-pst-2s be-pres-2s
'You have remained there.'

(87) (a) *ēn* *es-k-an* *ra'-ck-an.*
I-nom break-prt-1s be-pst-1s
'I had broken (it).'

(b) *nīn* *es-k-ai* *ra'-ck-ai.*
you-nom break-prt-2s be-pst-2s
'You had broken (it).'

Morphological analysis confirms that the two examples in (86) are SVFs: each component of the construction is in its own right a finite verb. These particular examples illustrate the present perfect tense in Kuṛux, a form whose morphological structure agrees in every detail but one with the attested present perfect in Parji and the reconstructed forms in Konḍa and Pengo. It differs in that it uses the etymologically unrelated auxiliary verb *bē'ena* 'be' in place of the inherited Dravidian auxiliary *manna* 'be'. Steever (1984) shows that copular verbs borrowed into Kuṛux from Indo-Aryan have gradually restricted and supplanted the inherited Dravidian verbs. What matters here is that the structural pattern of the present perfect, which is a pure Dravidian SVF, has been preserved here.

The two examples in (87) illustrate the past perfect tense form in Kuṛux. Though it is an auxiliary compound verb, it falls short of being a SVF in one respect: the main verb is a past participle that is inflected for subject-verb agreement, and not an independently finite verb form. The main verb *es-k-an* 'I, having broken' in *es-k-an ra'-ck-an* 'I had broken' in (87) b consists of the verb base *es-* 'break', the past participle marker *-k* (*e*) and the personal ending of the first person singular *-an*. It is possible that in the pre-history of Kuṛux this form was a finite verb since *-k*(*e*) seems to be an allomorph of the past tense morpheme in some varieties of Malto. That speculation, however, has no direct bearing on the synchronic analysis of this form in modern Kuṛux: the form *eskan* cannot appear in the position specially designated for finite predicates, and is therefore non-finite. Table 20 is compiled from my own field-notes, and gives a fuller paradigm of this participial construction, illustrating the past perfect tense form of *kāl-*/*ker-* 'go'. Note that in order to be a full-fledged SVF the main verb would have to bear the past tense marker, giving rise to the non-occurring forms **ker-ck-an rah-ck-an*, etc.

TABLE 20: The past perfect in Kuṛux, *kāl-*/*ker-* 'go', in which the main verb is a conjugated participle

	Singular	Plural
1	*ker-k-an rah-ck-an*	*ker-k-am rah-ck-am*
2m	*ker-k-ai rah-ck-ai*	*ker-k-ar rah-ck-ar*
2f	*kir-k-i rah-ck-i*	
3	*ker-k-as rah-c-as*	*ker-k-ar rah-c-ar*

We shall leave this participial construction for the time being, and concentrate on true SVFs.

Lexical Compound Verbs and Co-ordinate Structures

Bloch (1946: 45) quotes some examples of the SVF in Kuṛux, of which one is reproduced below.

(88) *ās ī punā nalakh karnē urmin xind-y-as piṭ-y-as.*
he-nom this new work about all buy-pst-3s kill-pst-3s
'Because of his new work (i.e., salary), he bought up everything'.

The SVF *xind-y-as piṭ-y-as* 'he bought up' in (88) consists of the two finite verbs *xind-y-as* 'he bought' and *piṭ-y-as* 'he killed'. The whole SVF appears to be a lexical compound verb, or perhaps an auxiliary compound verb that marks completion of action.

Vesper (1971), Ekka (1972, 1978), and Gordon (1974) record a variety of SVFs which are illustrated below.

(89)(a) *karata-c-ar ci-c-ar.*
carry across-pst-3p give-pst-3p
'They chased (someone) away.'

(b) *bas-c-ar ker-c-ar.*
inhabit-pst-3p go-pst-3p
'They settled in.'

(c) *ārg-i-ar bar-c-ar.*
climb-pst-3p come-pst-3p
'They attacked.'

(d) *hā-r-c-ar ker-c-ar.*
defeat-rfx-pst-3p go-pst-3p
'They got defeated.'

The exact classification of the SVFs in (89), taken from Vesper (1971), is somewhat difficult. While (89)b and d might be interpreted as auxiliary compound verbs signalling completion of action, (89)a and c should be treated as lexical compound verbs because the meaning of the whole compound is not predictable from the meaning of the parts.

Ekka (1978) describes SVFs that resemble those already collected by Bloch and Vesper.

(90)(a) *ēn nīn ender nan-d-ay capp-d-ay anne*
I-nom you-nom what do-pres-2s hurry-pres-2s like
nan-d-an capp-d-an.
do-pres-1s hurry-pres-1s
'What(ever) you do quickly, I do quickly.'

(b) *ēn mox-d-an capp-d-an ā alas hik-d-an.*
I-nom eat-pres-1s hurry-pres-1s that man-nom be-pres-1s
'I am the man who eats quickly.'

(c) *xall tara kāl-age eRpati ur-kh-as ābīrim*
field towards go-inf house-loc come out-pst-3s that time
cēp bar-c-a cic-c-a.
rain-nom come-pst-3s give-pst-3s
'When he came out of the house to go to the field, the rain fell.'

(d) *rāj narainas indirā gāndhin harabā-c-as cic-c-as.*
Raj Narayan-nom Indira Gandhi-acc defeat-pst-3s give-pst-3s
'Raj Narayan soundly defeated Indira Gandhi.'

(e) *jōxar emhae eRpati cānum boṅ-ṅg-ar kā-n-ar.*
servants our house-abl yearly run-pres-3p go-pres-3p
'Servants run away from our house every year.'

(f) *ēn jōx man-d-an ciʔ-d-an.*
I-nom servant be-pres-1s do temporarily-pres-1s
'I am becoming a servant temporarily.'

(g) *ḍhiba māl ci-ʔ-oe hole ghoron ho-ʔ-on kā-l-on.*
money not give-fut-2s if horse take-fut-1s go-fut-1s
'If you do not give money, I'll take the horse away.'

The auxiliary verb *capp-* 'hurry', whose semantics resembles the Tamil auxiliary verb *taḷḷa* 'push' (Steever 1983: 470-78), appears in two SVFs in (90)a and in one SVF in (90)b, where it is embedded in a relative clause. The completive auxiliary verbs *ci-* 'give' and *kāl-/ker-* 'go' appear in SVFs in (90)c and d, and (90)e and g, respectively. Finally, the auxiliary verb *ciʔ-* 'do temporarily' appears in the SVF in (90)f. In each SVF in these examples, the tense markers and personal endings of the two component verbs agree.

Other constructions in Kuṛux also show this same reduplication of suffixes between two members of a compound verb. But here the suffixes are typical of non-finite verbs, rather than finite. Consider the two following sentences.

(91) (a) *ēn mox-na cap-na ālan hik-d-an.*
I-nom eat-adnp hurry-adnp man-nom be-pres-1s
'I am the man who eats hurriedly'.

(b) *ēn bar-num capp-num īri-k-an cappi-k-an.*
I-nom come-when hurry-when see-pst-1s hurry-pst-1s
'As I came quickly, I saw it quickly.'

In comparing (90)b with (91)a and b, we see that both members of the compound verb bear the inflections that the grammatical context imposes on them, rather than the auxiliary verb alone. This suggests the possibility that SVFs in Kuṛux belong to a larger set of verbal constructions in which all component members of the construction must assume the inflections imposed on them by the context. If that is so, then SVFs may be generated by means other than Rule (45). Limitations of space prevent us from exploring this possibility further, but it is not cause for alarm because we have already suggested that echo compound formation is responsible for the creation of some SVFs. What matters is that the grammar of Kuṛux permits the occurrence of multiple finite verbs in a single construction, and to this extent retains the common Dravidian heritage of SVFs. We cannot yet ascertain whether the rules responsible for the constructions in (91)a and b are extensions of Rule (45), or simply have another origin.

Gordon (1974) provides us with further examples of this productive pattern of SVFs in Kuṛux.

(92)(a) *bijj-i-a* *ker-a.*
dawn-pst-3s go-pst-3s
'It dawned.'

(b) *banṭhu-s* *nēṭas* *māyya* *ukk-i-as* *cic-c-as.*
Banthu-nom Neta upon sit-pst-3s give-pst-3s
'Banthu sat on top of Neta.'

(c) *manku-s* *put-r-as* *cic-c-as.*
Mankhu-nom vomit-rfx-pst-3s give-pst-3s
'Mankhu vomited (unexpectedly).'

(d) *banṭhu-s* *mankhus-in* *lāw-c-as* *le* *hoc-c-as.*
Banthu-nom Mankhu-acc strike-pst-3s pcl take-pst-3s
'Banthu struck Mankhu (unexpectedly, the speaker didn't think he could do it).'

(e) *jhannar* *xessan* *xaṭṭ-r-ar* *ke-r-ar.*
workmen paddy-acc divide-rfx-pst-3p go-pst-3p
'The workmen divided the paddy among themselves.'

(f) *jorse* *pīt-r-a* *ke-r-a.*
loudly fart-rfx-pst-3s go-pst-3s
'Someone farted loudly.'

(g) *āku* *duniadāri* *kudd-i-as* *nan-j-as.*
now world travel-pst-3s do-pst-3s
'So now he has been travelling around the world.'

The structure of the SVFs in these examples is the same as that of the preceding set. The only remark that we need to make here concerns the

SVF in (92)d: the auxiliary verb *hoc-* 'take' requires the presence of the emphatic particle *le* between the main and auxiliary verbs, in much the same way that the past and present progressive negative forms of Ollari require the interpolation of the union vowel *-i-*.

Related Forms and Rules

Kuṛux has a grammatical process similar to Affix-Truncation, and it has compound verbs that utilize the bare verb base of the main verb. Both these ingredients have been observed to appear alongside of SVFs in a number of languages. As far as I can tell, Affix-Truncation in Kuṛux applies only in the past perfect paradigm where it removes the final consonant of the personal ending on the main verb. The following alternations may thus be observed.

(93) (a)	*ēn*	*ker-k-an*	*rah-ck-an.*
	I-nom	go-prt-1s	be-pst-1s
	'I had gone.'		
(b)	*ēn*	*ker-k-a*	*rah-ck-an.*
	I-nom	go-prt-tpe	be-pst-1s
	'I had gone.'		

(94) (a)	*ēm*	*ker-k-am*	*rah-ck-am.*
	we-nom	go-prt-1p	be-pst-1p
	'We had gone.'		
(b)	*ēm*	*ker-k-a*	*rah-ck-am.*
	we-nom	go-prt-1tpe	be-pst-1p
	'We had gone.'		

This pattern of Affix-Truncation resembles that in Konḍa, where it whittles down the repeated personal ending on the main verb to its initial vowel.

At least one Kuṛux auxiliary verb, *nakʔr-* 'do to each other', combines with the bare verb base of the main verb to form an auxiliary compound verb. Two variants occur: in one the reflexive marker *-r-* appears on the main verb, in the other on the auxiliary.

(95) (a)	*nīn*	*awr*	*ālas*	*ews-r*	*nakʔ-d-ar.*
	you-nom	and	man-nom	touch-rfx-bvb	do-pres-2p
	'You and the man touch each other.'				
(b)	*nīn*	*awr*	*ālas*	*ēra*	*nakʔ-r-d-ar.*
	you-nom	and	man-nom	see-bvb	do-rfx-pres-2p
	'You and the man see each other.'				

Though Ekka (1972) does not gloss it, the verb *nakʔr-* 'do to each other' probably comes from the verb *nal-/nan-* 'do' and a reflexive auxiliary verb **kVr* which is contracted from **koḷ* 'hold' (*DEDR* 2151). If this is so, then the reflexive auxiliary *nak?r-* 'do to each other' is itself cognate with reflexive verbs in Telugu with the auxiliary *kon* 'hold' (see Chapter IV).

Some of the Kuṛux SVFs we have examined are certainly cognate with SVFs in other Dravidian languages: the present perfect forms in (86) and the SVFs with auxiliaries like *kāl-/ker-* 'go' and *ci-* 'give' represent common Dravidian SVFs.

3. MALTO

Like Kuṛux, Malto has both true SVFs and participial constructions that resemble them in marking subject-verb agreement. Of the two, the latter seems to be more common. Although the participles that mark subject-verb agreement are non-finite in that they cannot occur in the position specially designated for finite predicates, they may well descend from earlier finite verb forms. If that is so, then the complex verbal constructions in which they appear, descend from SVFs.

Careful study of Malto turns up a small, yet significant set of SVFs recorded in the available texts. The number of SVFs is expected to increase proportionally as more texts are collected and published.

(96) (a) *ājogyeh* *men-j-ah* *aw-ḍ-ah.*
mendicant-nom hear-pst-3sm speak-pst-3sm
'The mendicant listened and spoke.'

(b) *ājogyeh* *men-j-ah* *aw-ḍ-l-ah.*
mendicant-nom hear-pst-3sm speak-pst-neg-3sm
'The mendicant listened and didn't speak.'

(c) *bita-k-ar* *o-c-ar* *mand-ar.*
cook-pst-3p take-pst-3p plant-pst-3p
'They cooked, took, and planted them.'

(d) *ketaweh* *inor* *din* *ṭunḍ-ot* *ek-d-ah* *bar-d-ah.*
farmer-nom now daily see-inf go-pres-3sm come-pres-3sm
'The farmer is going and coming everyday to see.'

(e) *sardarni-nnte* *binḍ-ka-h* *baj-o-c-ah*
chief-abl begin-prt-3sm strike-take-pst-3sm
baj-ondr-ah.
strike-bring-pst-3sm
'Starting with the chief, he went on beating (them)'

(f) *mand-ko* *siyareʒ* *maqa* *ek-k-iʒ* *goṭen* *i*
plant-cond jackal-nom at night go-prt-3sn all emp
tūr-a *tūr-a* *min* *oṅ-k-i* *ār* *manday-c-ar*
dig-prt dig-prt eat-bvb finish-prt-3sn they plant-pst-3p

manday-c-ar *aḍno* *erg̣* *erg̣*
plant-pst-3p there defecate-bvb defecate-bvb
top-ce *ojr-aǯ.*
bury-prt flee-pst-3sn
'When they planted, the jackal went at night, dug up and ate (the arums), and wherever they (had) planted, he buried his droppings there, and went away.'

(g) *chi-y-en* *bichr-en.*
give-fut-1s distribute-fut-1s
'I shall give (it) away.'

In examples (96)a and b every verb is formally finite; therefore the two constructions are SVFs. They are co-ordinate verb constructions, as is example (96)c. The balance SVF *ekdah bardah* 'he moves about' in (96)c consists of the two finite verbs *ekdah* 'he goes' and *bardah* 'he comes'. The iterative SVF *mandaycar mandaycar* 'they planted and planted' in (96) arises through the reduplication of a single finite verb form. The SVF *baj-ocah baj-ondrah* 'he beat and beat' in (96)e is a complex balance compound verb: each component consists of the lexeme *baj* 'strike' and a finite verb based on *oc-* 'take' or *ondr-* 'bring'. It resembles the Konḍa examples (74)f and (77), as well as the Pengo example (78) d and Parji example (82)b. Note that the suffixes within any given SVF never contrast (with the exception of (96)b where one verb, but not the other incorporates the negative marker).

Related Forms and Rules

Droese (1884) and Mahapatra (1979) record two participles in Malto, one perfective (prf prt) and the other imperfective (impf prt), which mark subject-verb agreement by means of personal endings. The perfective participle is formed by suffixing *-k* (*a*) to the verb base; the imperfective participle by suffixing *-n*(*a*). Personal endings are subsequently suffixed to the participles. It should be noted that in the Sawriya dialect *-k-* is an allomorph of the past tense morpheme, and *-n-* an allomorph of the present tense morpheme. This suggests that the perfective and imperfective participles inflected for personal endings descend from past and present finite verbs, respectively. In other dialects, however, neither participle can appear in the position specially designated for finite predicates. The use of these participles is governed by a same-subject condition: the personal endings of the conjugated participle must agree with that of the following verb.

(97) (a) *ēn* *ţūnḍ-k-en* *bech-k-en.*
I-nom see-prf prt-1s be-pst-1s
'I had seen.'

(b) *āh* *bar-c-ah* *atheno* *taṅgḍoh* *ek-k-eh* *bechch-ah.*
he-nom come-pst-3s then brother-nom go-prf prt-3s be-pst-3s
'When he came, his brother had gone.'

(98) (a) *ēca-k-ah* *ḍaṛond* *bēdalāgo* *laṭin* *otr-ah.*
bind-prf prt-3sm long one large stick take-pst-3sm
'He took out a long, large stick, having bound (them).'

(b) *bita-k-ar* *o-c-ar* *mand-ar.*
cook-prf prt-3p take-pst-3p plant-pst-3p
'Having cooked (them), they took and planted (them).'

(99) (a) *ār* *bed-n-er* *bed-n-er* *bar-n-ar.*
they search-impf prt-3p search-impf prt-3p come-pres-3p
'They come searching and searching.'

(b) *ār* *olg-n-er* *paṛ-n-er* *aw-ḍ-ar.*
they cry-impf prt-3p shout-impf prt-3p speak-pst-3p
'They shouted and howled.'

(c) *ād* *bong-n-iʔ* *ek-y-aʔ.*
she run-impf prt-3f go-pst-3f
'She ran away.'

In the past perfect tense forms in (97) the main verb appears in the perfective participle while the auxiliary verb appears in the past tense: it structurally resembles the Kuṛux past perfect in (87) and Table 20. The perfective participle appears in the co-ordinate verb constructions in (98). The imperfective participle appears in the compound verb constructions in (99). Comparison with other structures in our survey suggests that these conjugated participles occupy a position between the plain compound verb and the true SVF.

Mahapatra (1979) observes that the perfective conjugated participles have two variants. In the first the final consonant of the personal ending is removed from the participle, resulting in a truncated personal ending; in the second both the personal ending and the participial morpheme are stripped away, leaving only the bare verb base.

(100) (a) *ēn* *nāra-n* *anḍ-a(n)* *coṛnt-an.*
I-nom ghost-acc find-prf prt-tpe be startled-pst-1s
'I was startled by finding a ghost.'

(b) *ṭāṭge* *panj-e(ʔ)* *cogr-aʔ.*
mango-nom ripen-prf prt-tpe fall-pst-3n
'The mango ripened and fell.'

(101) (a)

ēn	*ondr*	*ondr*	*bāṭ-y-an.*
I-nom	bring-bvb	bring-bvb	distribute-fut-1s

'I shall bring and distribute (all of it).'

(b)

āh	*ḍarin-ḍaban*	*oc*	*oc*	*te-y-ah.*
he-nom	clothes	take-bvb	take-bvb	throw-pst-3s

'He took up the clothes and threw them out.'

In (100)a the conjugated perfective participle *anḍ-an* 'I having found' alternates with the truncated form *anḍ-a* 'ibid'. A similar alternation occurs in (100)b. Such alternations seem to be possible only when the participle and finite verb directly abut one another, otherwise only the fully conjugated participle can be used. Additionally, when the perfective participle and finite verb are adjacent, both the participial morpheme and personal ending of the former may be deleted, as in (101). The truncation of the personal endings of the conjugated participles in (100) corresponds exactly to the same phenomenon in the Kuṛux examples (93) and (94). That personal endings appear on conjugated participles, and that they may undergo Affix-Truncation are two additional arguments for the claim that these participles ultimately descend from finite verb forms.

Further exploration of Malto syntax would help us to define more clearly the rules that generate SVFs and conjugated participles. This research should also locate the rules that generate the SVF within the body of agreement rules that affect predicate nominals, predicate adjectives, and even the two postpositions *lagca* 'for' and *orgi* 'until'.

4. BRAHUI

Brahui has at least one SVF: it is a compound verb in which both the main verb and the auxiliary verb *hin-* 'go' bear the same inflections. The auxiliary seems to convey the notions of suddenness or completion of the action of the main verb.

(102) (a)

kask	*hinā.*
die-pst-3m	go-pst-3m

'He died (outright).'

(b)

ī	*xalkunuṭ*	*hinanuṭ-ta.*
I	thrash-pres prf-1s	go-pres prf-1s^{sub}-3m^{obj}

'I have thrashed him (soundly).'

(c)

num	*xalkure*	*hināre.*
you	thrash-pst-2p	go-pst-2p

'You thrashed (soundly).'

(d) *hināṭ* *ki* *tēnā* *hullīe* *halēv* *kanā*
go-pst-1s that my horse fetch-fut-1s but
rasēgān *must* *kaskas* *hināsas.*
reach before die-pst-3n go-pst-3n
'I went to fetch my horse, but before I reached it, it was stone dead.'

(e) *tēnā* *xarase* *taf,* *kanā* *beite* *kulle*
your bullock tie-imp or all grass
kunēk *kaik.*
eat-fut-3n go-fut-3n
'Tie your bullock, or it will eat up all the grass.'

All the compound verbs in (101) meet our definition of the SVF, since both the main and auxiliary verbs are finite forms in their own right. The semantics of *hin-* 'go' resembles that of Tamil *pōka* 'go' (Steever 1983 : 494-99).

5. SUMMARY

All three languages of the North Dravidian subgroup have SVFs in abundance. Emeneau (1980: 322) compares the Brahui forms in (102) with the cognate forms in Kuṛux that use the completive auxiliary verb *kāl-/ker* 'go' e.g. (89)b and d, (90)e, (92)a and d. (The Brahui cognate of Kuṛux *kāl-/ker-, ka-*, appears only in the future paradigm, and is subject to suppletion elsewhere.) Emeneau's comparison led him to draw the conclusion that since "such inflection of both main and auxiliary verb does not occur...in general Dravidian, ... it is very probable that we have here a North Dravidian innovation." The severe restrictions against multiple finite verbs in the Dravidian sentence, as embodied in Rule (44), may have contributed to this judgment. However, the evidence adduced in the three previous chapters proves beyond the shadow of a doubt that the SVF is an integral part of common Dravidian syntax, and may accordingly be reconstructed to the proto-language. Consequently, the claim that SVFs are innovations within North Dravidian must be revised in favor of a demonstration that they belong to a common Dravidian heritage, and are thus retentions in the north subgroup.

Our survey shows that North Dravidian languages retain SVFs which strongly resemble SVFs in the three other subgroups. The SVF may be an auxiliary compound verb, as the Kuṛux present perfect; a lexical compound verb, as the Malto balance compound in (96)e; or a co-ordinate verb construction, as in (96)a. Perhaps the most obvious departure from the common Dravidian pattern is the presence of conjugated participles in Kuṛux and Malto (although Koṇḍa might be heading in this direction). These forms, which stand between the plain compound verb and the full-fledged SVF, have no obvious cognates in the rest of the family. However, the similarity of the perfective and imperfective participle morphemes to the past and present tense morphemes, respectively, suggests an origin in the set of finite verbs. This conclusion is further buttressed by the fact that the perfective conjugated participle undergoes Affix-Truncation, and alternates with the bare verb base in plain compound verbs. The agreement rules of North Dravidian have grown so that they now apply to predicate nominals, predicate adjectives, and even two postpositions in Malto. The Kuṛux data suggests that the agreement among the suffixes of a compound verb may be the result of a very general rule that reduplicates verb inflections. Even though some North Dravidian SVFs may be generated by these general rules, they nevertheless conform to the pattern of SVFs that has been established throughout the Dravidian family.

Chapter Seven

THE SERIAL VERB FORMATION IN DRAVIDIAN SYNTAX

1. CATALOGUES, PATTERNS, AND RULES

The four preceding chapters in effect constitute an annotated catalogue of the SVF, organized according to subgroup for comparative purposes. The decision to introduce so much empirical data through this catalogue stems from two related concerns. The first and most obvious one is that a substantial body of evidence is required to fuel the grammatical arguments concerning the structure, variation, and history of the SVF. It is only by appeal to concrete examples, and particularly to the patterns they imply, that we can begin to determine the exact role of the SVF in common Dravidian grammar. Yet we have no comparative handbook to consult for this specific purpose, no seminal articles, nor even relevant sections of individual grammars.[1] The catalogue is primarily intended to supply their lack. The second and less obvious concern is to combat the deeply engrained attitude that is responsible for the virtual silence surrounding the SVF in the Dravidian linguistic literature. I hazard the opinion that certain assumptions about the extensive role of the plain compound verb and the limited distribution of finite predicates in the construction of the Dravidian sentence have forced the SVF into a blind-spot. These assumptions seem to have unconsciously conditioned Dravidian linguists against perceiving the SVF, much less analyzing it in a systematic way. Since it so baldly contravenes the constraint against multiple finite predicates, it is dismissed as un-Dravidian or worse. Any grammatical analysis of the SVF naturally presupposes its existence, a claim which under different circumstances in the history of Dravidian linguistics might have seemed trivial. But since the SVF falls so far outside the set of constructions that tradition has received as unexceptionably Dravidian, extra effort is required just to overcome the expectations against its discovery. Indeed, the sheer weight of the catalogue is largely meant to demonstrate the existence of the SVF over and against the predisposition not to perceive it. If this book confirms the existence of the SVF in the Dravidian languages, it will have succeeded in its single most important goal.

Once the existence of the SVF is admitted, its analysis may be undertaken. The catalogue of examples implies a set of structural patterns which in turn implies a rudimentary theory of the SVF. From the catalogue emerge certain recurring patterns, and from these patterns, explicit rules. These patterns and rules, made by induction, may be applied as tests against the predictions, made by deduction, about the SVF at the beginning of Chapter III. Individual examples from the catalogue overwhelmingly confirm these predictions in their capacity as a preliminary theory of the SVF.

The majority of SVFs prove to be compound verbs, while the rest consist of co-ordinate verb constructions that mimic the compound verb in its gross structural properties. It is known on independent grounds (Benveniste 1965, Steever 1983) that the compound verb, no matter how internally complex, has just one logical subject, hence just one set of subject-verb agreement features. Chapter III accordingly predicted that no contrast should ever arise among the personal endings of the individual verbs within a single SVF. And in fact none of the examples in the catalogue ever exhibits such a contrast. This observation includes co-ordinate verb constructions, which must satisfy a same-subject constraint in order to be SVFs (even though they need not otherwise obey such a constraint, e.g. (11)a, (12)a. Inspection of the catalogue also reveals that the SVF alternates with plain compound verbs, or *mutatis mutandis* plain co-ordinate verb constructions, in one stage of a single language, between two stages of the same language, or across different languages. This alternation, expressed by Rule (45), integrates the SVF further into Dravidian grammar. The SVF is subject to the same kind of taxonomies and historical development as plain compound verbs. Those SVFs which are compound verbs have the same subdivisions as plain compound verbs: auxiliary and lexical. Examples of the auxiliary SVF may be cited in the negative conjugation, the present perfect tense, benefactive voice, and completive aspect. Several well-known, independently attested kinds of lexical compound verb also appear in our catalogue of the SVF: iterative, balance, and echo compound verbs appear there as robustly as elsewhere. Contracted SVFs and truncated SVFs make use of common historical processes such as Auxiliary Contraction and Auxiliary Verb Deletion. The SVF may be synchronically generated by at least three different rules: Rule (45), Reduplication, and Echo Compound Formation can all on occasion give rise to the SVF. Nevertheless their output is consistent in its gross structure, which prompts us to suggest that output constraints on surface structure, such as Rule (44), must guide their application. The SVF will in short order be integrated into such a rule. We see that the consistent and recurring patterns, the alternations with kindred constructions, the similarity of taxonomies and historical development, the exploitation of independently attested rules, and the conformity to general output constraints all argue in favor of the integration and rule-governed status of the SVF within common Dravidian grammar.

While the examples in the catalogue confirm the general predictions of Chapter III concerning the SVF, further inspection reveals even more specific patterns. Although the general patterns are repeated throughout the four primary subgroups, it is even more telling that individual SVFs are found to resurface in different languages. The present perfect tense form with the auxiliary verb **man* 'be' (*DEDR* 4778) appears with the same morphological structure in pre-Tamil, pre-Koṇḍa, pre-Pengo, Parji, and pre-Kuṛux. The negative conjugation with the auxiliary verb **ā* 'become' (*DEDR* 333), or its suppletive variants, appears in Old Tamil, Old Kannaḍa, pre-Kota, pre-Toda, Old Telugu, Muria Gonḍi, pre-Koṇḍa, pre-Kolami, and Ollari. Their distribution is sufficiently broad to warrant their reconstruction to Proto-Dravidian. The catalogue also contains echo SVFs based on the echo syllable **ki-/*pV-*, which may be reconstructed to the proto-language, too. The great historical depth of these SVFs is a strong argument in favor of their essential Dravidian status.

These persistently recurring patterns demand an explicit and systematic treatment in comparative Dravidian grammar. Apart from Emeneau (1980) and Agesthialingom (1983), however, most previous attempts to explain the presence of the SVF in Dravidian have yielded thoroughly uninspiring results. When it is not simply ignored, it is variously treated as a borrowing from Indo-Aryan, a performance error, a freakish idiom, a slip of the tongue, or a stylistic conceit. These are mere labels, not systematic explanations of the SVF. As such they make no coherent contribution to comparative grammar.

None of these approaches to the SVF seriously addresses the grammatical questions that are raised by its presence in the Dravidian languages. All of them beg one of the most important questions of modern linguistics: what underlying structural principles of language make a certain form or rule possible? We may ask in the present case what facet of Dravidian syntax would permit the SVF to be borrowed from Indo-Aryan and grafted onto the body of native syntactic rules? Into what existing structural grooves could the tongue slip and thereby produce the SVF with such regularity? What formal apparatus do speakers of the Dravidian languages possess that would let a stylistic mannerism spread so rapidly and penetrate to the heart of the auxiliary verb system? These then are the kinds of questions that need to be asked. Even if it were protested against all our evidence that the SVF originated outside Dravidian, we would still have to ask how the borrowing language could even begin to assimilate so alien a structure. We would still have to determine what native rules had assumed the responsibility for generating the borrowed structure, the SVF. That is of course tantamount to writing a synchronic description of the SVF, one which by definition accepts it as an integral part of the language. No matter whether it is native or borrowed, a commonplace expression or a stylistic conceit, a grammatical convention or a performance error, the SVF and its grammar must be synchronically analyzed. This task logically takes precedence over all attempts to ascertain its historical or areal source. We must discover the morphological and syntactic processes that generate the SVF, and their role in the larger grammatical system.

Chapter I argues that finiteness is a syntactic property that is morphologically interpreted. Formation rules determine the syntax of finite expressions, while agreement rules interpret them according to the morphological parameters of the language. Since the definition of the SVF mentions the property of finiteness, its analysis must take morphological and syntactic properties into account.

Consider first the syntactic processes that give rise to the SVF and how they are embedded in and constrained by the rest of Dravidian syntax. Although three different rules have been shown to give rise to the SVF, their application and their output are constrained by rules such as (44). It is in fact a surface structure formation rule that serves as an output constraint on Dravidian sentences. The extent to which the SVF simply and directly interacts with such a rule proves to be a good measure of the degree to which it is integrated into Dravidian grammar. Thus, Rule (44) may be conservatively revised to accommodate the SVF.

The Final Revision

Chapter III introduced the distinction between functionally and formally finite predicates as a means of integrating the SVF in a revision of Rule (44). A form is functionally finite if and only if it occupies one of the specially designated positions for finite predicates; otherwise, it is functionally non-finite. A form is considered formally finite if it satisfies two conditions. It must be a verb inflected for tense and a personal ending, marking subject-verb agreement.[2] It must derive its personal endings from a functionally finite verb that appears in the same construction as the head. Since the individual examples in the catalogue confirm these predictions, we may proceed with our revision of Rule (44). It consists in a simple substitution: replace the term finite predicate everywhere with the term functionally finite predicate. The revision preserves the essence of Rule (44), while admitting the possibility of the SVF.

(103) RULE FOR THE DISTRIBUTION OF FINITE PREDICATES

(a) Each Dravidian sentence has exactly $n+1$ FUNCTIONALLY finite predicates, where n stands for the number of FPEs and 1 for the RDFP.

(b) The functionally finite predicate in the RDFP occurs highest and rightmost in the root clause, commands all other predicates, and is itself commanded by none. Each FPE induces a DDFP. The functionally finite predicate in each DDFP occurs highest and rightmost in the sentence that c-commands the FPE, commands all other predicates, and is itself commanded by none.

(c) Each functionally finite predicate may be accompanied by indefinitely many FORMALLY finite verbs, if it belongs to the set of expressions that govern the application of rules which generate the SVF.

(d) Each formally finite verb occurs in a construction, the head of which is a functionally finite verb. Its morphological interpretation is assigned by that functionally finite verb: it incorporates tense, mood, or negation, and a personal ending congruent with the functionally finite verb's.

(e) All other predicates are non-finite, functionally and formally.

According to Rule (103) finiteness is a syntactic property: it inheres in certain constituent structures selected by the various clauses of the rule. Moreover, two kinds of finiteness are defined in Rule (103). Functional finiteness is immediately derived from the gross constituent structure of the sentence, and is associated with the particular sites identified in (103)a and b. It guides the application of subject-predicate agreement rules to the forms that occupy those sites. Formal finiteness, on the other hand, is derived from the dependence relation that obtains between a verbal construction and its head. The morphological interpretation of the components in such a construction is made to vary directly with the head, which is a functionally finite verb. Thus formal finiteness presupposes functional finiteness, a fact which is inscribed in the structure of Rule (103).

Just as the term FPE is used in Rule(103) to cover a wide range of constructions that crucially refer to functional finiteness, the term SVF is used to cover the various constructions that refer to formal finiteness. Included in this diverse set are the auxiliary compound verb, the lexical compound verb with all its subclasses, and the co-ordinate verb construction. Rule (103) is not primarily intended to define such leading concepts as FPE, SVF, or matrix-complement structure. It is principally designed to constrain their use of finite predicates. Other grammatical principles are needed to define the individual constructions.

Since Rule (103) is schematic, appeal must be made to other grammatical rules and structures to interpret it fully. Note 11, Chapter I, observes that an independent algorithm is available to select the auxiliary verb in any auxiliary compound verb so that it bears the inflections that the grammatical context imposes, and not the main verb (Steever1983). The number of FPEs is determined by counting the surface, not underlying occurrences. This practise accords equal importance to FPEPs that are transformationally inserted and to those that are base-generated. It also takes into account the number of FPECs that result from the application of Conjunction-Spreading, even though logical structure may have one conjunction or quantifier where the corresponding surface structure has many.

Similar steps must be taken to ensure the proper interpretation of the SVF. In light of our analysis of finiteness in Rule (103), the definition of the SVF may be simplified: it is any construction that contains a formally finite verb. Rule (103) supplies the rest: a formally finite verb must always be accompanied and governed by a functionally finite verb. This accurately describes all of those constructions that consist of two or more verb forms with essentially congruent personal endings. The word-formation rules further assist in the interpretation: they tell us that a verb form that incorporates a personal ending also incorporates a verbal category such as tense, mood, or negation. Here as above, we may have to invoke independent structures to complete our interpretation of the SVF. If, for example, the functionally finite verb in a SVF happens to be an auxiliary verb, we may then appeal to the theory of the auxiliary compound verb to locate the formally finite verb, which happens here to be the main verb. In a language like Konḍa Rule (45) appears to apply without any restrictions (before the application of Affix-Truncation): every compound verb and co-ordinate verb construction may be a (truncated) SVF. In Muria Gonḍi, on the other hand, it is lexically restricted so that only the negative auxiliary verb *ava* 'become' can trigger its application.

Further syntactic analysis of the SVF must draw out the implications of these schematic rules, the better to determine the exact form of the various rules that generate the SVF, as well as the limits on their application. The different restrictions in Konḍa and Pengo on the application of Rule (45) have just illustrated this point. Let us take Echo Compound Formation as another example. Not only do the echo syllables vary from one language to the next, but so do the exact formulation of the rule and the constraints on its use. It applies freely to past tense forms in Telugu, but only with reservations in Tamil. In the Kannaḍa contingent tense, but perhaps not its Telugu cognate, it may echo either the bare verb case or the fully inflected verb. Affix-Truncation may apply optionally in Pengo, but obligatorily in Konḍa; it may remove part of the repeated ending in Konḍa, or all of it in Classical Tamil.

Nothing could be easier at this point than to multiply the grammatical studies that need to be undertaken for a more profound understanding of the SVF, but they would certainly swell this volume to several times its present size. Pending new research and re-evaluation of the old, based on our preliminary study of the SVF, we must content ourselves with schematic rules, general constraints, and the broad outlines of the theory of the SVF. All of them may serve as guidelines for comparative research, as well as the study of the SVF in individual languages. It is expected that the accumulation of new material and interpretations will help transform this research program into a full-fledged theory. What matters for the present, however, is that the SVF should in all its shapes conform to Rule (103). It is by virtue of participating in this rule firmly embedded in the larger grammatical system of the Dravidian languages. Rule (103) and the ancillary syntactic principles that are invoked to interpret it constitute the basis of a theory of the SVF.

Agreement

The syntactic analysis of the SVF, as expressed in Rule (103), rests on the distinction between functional and formal finiteness. This corresponds in turn to two different conceptions of the grammatical process of agreement, which is a means of morphologically interpreting a syntactic structure. Agreement requires that two distinct elements of a specified constituent be construed together by morphological means. When it interprets a functionally finite predicate, as determined by (103) a and b, the process of agreement marks the subject-predicate relation in the RDFP and DDFP morphologically. It imposes a relation of co-variation between subject and predicate with respect to the grammatical categories of person, number, and gender. In doing so it also redundantly marks the extreme right boundaries of the RDFP and DDFP. These seem to be the two primary functions of agreement. When it interprets a formally finite verb, on the other hand, agreement marks a subsidiary level of syntactic structure. It imposes congruent personal endings on the members of a verbal construction, and in doing so delineates the internal boundaries of that construction with respect to its head. It is clear that this secondary function of agreement has a more marked, more restricted range of application than the primary functions. This is due to the fact that every sentence necessarily has a subject-predicate relation, but may easily dispense with compound verbs and co-ordinate verb constructions. As the marked member of an opposition, the secondary use of agreement tends to be a good target of historical change, a prediction which is borne out by the fact that many Dravidian languages maintain the first and second clauses of (103), but lose the third and fourth.

No rule has been proposed to express the primary function of agreement. Although many studies assume that agreement is a matter of simply mapping the inherent features of person, number, and gender from the subject noun-phrase onto the designated predicate, it is in reality a far more complex process. Steever (1981, Chapter IV) shows that in Tamil agreement takes at least four different parameters into account: underlying person, surface number, intended gender, and honorification, all of which may vary independently of the others. It is for this reason that I have loosely defined agreement as a relation of co-variation between subject and predicate with respect to grammatical categories such as person, number, and gender (which often includes honorification). For our present purposes, the exact formulation of the primary function of agreement is unnecessary. Since the congruent personal endings in a SVF vary directly with the personal ending of the functionally finite predicate, Rule (45) is sufficient. Rule (45) does mechanically map the agreement features ascribed to the head of the construction onto its subsidiary members.

3. THE HISTORICAL DEVELOPMENT OF THE SVF

A certain tension exists between the primary and secondary functions of agreement: not only do they differ in markedness, but they interpret different surface constituent structures, as well.[3] In a language with SVFs a verb that marks tense and subject-verb agreement may at different times be used to interpret radically different structures. Such a verb form does not always occupy the specially designated positions for functionally finite predicates. In a language without SVFs, on the other hand, the distinction between functional and formal finiteness is neutralized in favor of the former so that every verb form that marks tense and subject-verb agreement is a functionally finite predicate. As noted earlier, the existence of this tension is not sufficient cause for a language to jettison its SVFs: it uses markedness relations to express the probability that a language will disencumber itself of its SVFs long before it gives up its functionally finite predicates. External conditions may set this process of historical loss in motion. It was observed above that the loss of Rule(45), SVFs, and ultimately (103)c and d seem to coincide with the loss of rules that inflect predicate nominals for subject-predicate agreement. I have not yet discovered any reason for this coincidence, and predict that more extensive analysis of subject-predicate agreement will help us to unravel this mystery. We shall see below that independent syntactic processes like Auxiliary Contraction and Auxiliary Verb Deletion may have profound influence on the historical development of the SVF.

Proto-Dravidian

Comparison of the various daughter languages permits us to reconstruct Rule (103) to the Proto-Dravidian era. The first two clauses accurately predict the distribution of finite predicates in sentences of the south, south-central, and central subgroups. Furthermore, internal and comparative reconstruction indicate that the divergence of the North Dravidian languages from Rule (103) a and b follows a line of development that exploits the class of FPEs and their role in the formulation of Rule (103). So many predicates and conjunctions have entered the set of FPEs that it lost its exceptional status, a change in markedness which naturally undermined the integrity of Rule (103) and, consequently, its ability to describe the role of finite and non-finite predicates in the construction of complex sentences. Finally, while it is easy to postulate the gradual expansion of the class of FPEs in the north subgroup, it is very hard to imagine how an essentially open class of FPEs could shrink in the three other subgroups so as to restrict the same set of etmya, viz. **ā* 'become' (*DEDR* 333) and **en* 'think, say' (*DEDR* 868), to the same unique function. Thus, (103)a and b belong to the proto-language.

The distribution of SVFs throughout the Dravidian family also requires the reconstruction of the third and fourth clauses of (103) to the proto-language. Auxiliary SVFs, lexical SVFs, and co-ordinate SVFs appear in all four of the primary subgroups. The SVF is therefore an integral part of Proto-Dravidian syntax.

The principles of comparative reconstruction also allow us to attribute Rule (45), Reduplication, and Echo Compound Formation, at least in schematic form, to the proto-language. Anyone of them can give rise to a SVF, and all three occur evenly distributed throughout the entire family. At least three specific SVFs may be reconstructed to Proto-Dravidian: the present perfect tense form with auxiliary **man* 'be' (*DEDR* 4778); the negative conjugation, particularly the past negative, with auxiliary **ā* 'become' (*DEDR* 333); and echo compounds with the echo syllable **ki-* 'shm-'. This leads to the conclusion that the SVF, which appears in about one-half of the daughter languages, is an intrinsic part of Proto-Dravidian syntax.

Subsequent Evolution

Not all of the daughter languages have preserved intact the Proto-Dravidian system of SVFs. Modern Malayāḷam has chosen the most radical course: the loss of subject-verb agreement rules there altogether precludes the possibility of creating SVFs. Since the functionally finite predicate is not morphologically interpreted with tense and personal endings, there is nothing for a formally finite verb to copy. Toda and Kota have lost their SVFs, as well. Although the past negative conjugation betrays traces of an earlier SVF, the constant and obligatory application of Affix-Truncation has helped to restructure the Word-Formation Rules for the past negative, rendering it opaque to its historical source (Steever 1987). The *ki*-Echo Compound Formation in Toda now echoes only the bare verb base, not the fully inflected finite form of a verb. Modern Tamil does maintain echo SVFs, even though most of the SVFs in the classical language were lost in the early medieval period. The trend towards the loss of the SVF appears in even the earliest stages of the language, as the contraction of the synthetic present perfect attests. Some languages like Parji have maintained a robust system of SVFs, and others like Koṇḍa have modified it slightly through the intervention of rules like Affix-Truncation. Still others like Muria Goṇḍi have extended the system of SVFs so that each innovated affirmative finite form is provided with a corresponding negative SVF.

Some fragmentary patterns in the development of the SVF emerge from the catalogue of the SVF. Those SVFs generated with the help of Rule (45) are lost before those generated by Reduplication or Echo Compound Formation. Both Modern Tamil and Kolami corroborate this claim. Processes like Affix-Truncation, Auxiliary Contraction, and Auxiliary Verb Deletion contribute to the gradual loss of the SVF: they help to mitigate the tension between functionally and formally finite verbs. The use of Affix-Truncation in Koṇḍa is instructive here. Only part of the finite verb's personal ending is truncated, so that a telltale vowel remains. All verbs except the one that occupies the specially designated position for finite predicates must undergo this process. The resulting system solves two problems with a single stroke. The truncated personal ending retains enough of its original shape to permit us to identify the different members of a SVF as constituents of a single construction. This preserves the secondary function of agreement to mark the constituents of a subsidiary construction. It also helps to ease the tension between formally and functionally finite verb forms, because truncated personal endings cannot appear where full personal endings can, and vice versa. The extension of this system to include all verbal constructions whose heads mark tense—finite or not—indicates to me that a certain balance has been struck between the two kinds of agreement. The creation of conjugated participles in Kuṛux and Malto seems to be a response to the same rationale. Agreement is still marked among the members of a compound verb or co-ordinate verb construction, but the conjugated participles may not trade places with functionally finite verbs, and vice versa.

The processes of Auxiliary Contraction, Auxiliary Verb Deletion, and Affix-Trunction help to bring about the same kind of historical compromise at the level of individual auxiliary SVFs. Auxiliary Contraction feeds subsequent rules that reduce and, ultimately, eliminate an auxiliary SVF, and along with it the tension between the two kinds of agreement. We have already seen this in the development of the past negative paradigm in Konḍa. The evolution of the present perfect paradigms in Pengo illustrates how the activity of these different processes actually brings about a reformulation of the word-formation rules for finite verbs so that they "capture" expressions formerly generated as SVFs (Steever 1984).

These kinds of solutions represent only the end-product of a long chain of linguistic strategies, only some of which are aimed at overcoming the tension between the two kinds of finiteness. These begin as optional rules, and only later develop into obligatory rules. Their optionality may be considered a means of dispersing the tension between the two kinds of finiteness. Consider the application of Auxiliary Verb Deletion to the auxiliary **man* 'be' (*DEDR* 4778), particularly to forms of the present perfect. Its application is optional in Kūi and Kūvi, obligatory in Pengo, but inoperative in Konḍa and Parji. This pattern suggests that it was optional in pre-Pengo. If it failed to apply to the present perfect forms there, the uncontracted SVF would continue to possess the repeated personal endings that symbolize the tension in finiteness. But if it did apply, it would lead to a reinterpretation of the repeated personal endings as parts of a single, discontinuous personal ending (Steever 1984). The optional application in pre-Pengo would have allowed the postulation of an alternation between the full and contracted forms of the present perfect, so that the contracted form might still be identified with the full SVF but obviate the tension between the two kinds of finiteness. It is only later that it became an obligatory rule. Comparison with Koṇḍa is instructive here because it chose an alternative path by making Affix-Truncation obligatory, whereas it remains optional in Pengo. Both developments conspire to the same end: they result in contracted SVFs, thereby reducing the tension between the two kinds of finiteness.

Auxiliary Verb Deletion does not apply of its own accord, but is fed by Auxiliary Contraction, which has a rationale of its own (Steever 1984, 1987). Auxiliary Contraction transforms the two parts of an auxiliary compound verb into a single word by replacing the word boundary that separate the main and auxiliary verbs with a simple morpheme boundary. Its application is intended to bring the form and function of a compound verb into synchronization. Although a compound verb consists of two individual verb forms, it functions as a single verb in the larger grammatical context. The transformation of two words into one is meant to match the form and function of the compound verb, at least on a superficial level. Auxiliary Contraction applies to SVFs and plain compound verbs alike. Contraction sets many other processes into action. Contracted compound verbs fail to conform to the word-formation rules for finite verbs: they are single words that have two lexical bases, two tense markers, and two personal endings. Other rules such as Auxiliary Verb Deletion are mustered to bring the contracted forms into conformity with the word-formation rules by whittling away some of the material in the contracted word. Auxiliary Verb Deletion is therefore as much a response to the need to maintain conformity with word-formation rules as it is a means of easing the tension between the two kinds of finiteness. What matters here is that the relative markedness between formal and functional finiteness helps to select the rules used to reduce the contracted forms, and to guide their application. Note that the subsequent rules usually apply so as to preserve the exponents of the functionally finite predicate, e.g. its tense marker and personal ending, at the expense of those on the formally finite verb. In two cases out of three in Pengo, it is the personal ending on the formally finite verb—the main verb—that is truncated. Therefore the relative markedness between formal and functional finiteness channels historical developments that are already in progress by weighting their outcome in favor of preserving functional finiteness. Thus, when we claim that such-and-such a process is applied to overcome the tension between the two kinds of finiteness, we are stating in effect that it follows the path of least resistence as described by their relative markedness.

These remarks are intended only to provide a general schema for the historical analysis of the SVF both in individual daughter languages and in specific branches of the Dravidian family. Many more articles and monographs must be dedicated to the study of specific examples before this general pattern is satisfactorily instantiated by particular cases. The relative markedness of formal and functional finiteness has been proposed as a general guideline to discover the particular processes responsible for the development of a given form. These markedness relations constrain diachronic developments of the SVF in much the same way that Rule (103) constrains the synchronic behavior of the rules that generate it. The two are indeed related since Rule (103) incorporates these markedness relations in its structure by defining formal finiteness in terms of functional finiteness.

3. PROSPECTS FOR THE FUTURE

We have established the presence of the SVF in fifteen of the Dravidian languages, analyzed its role in their grammars, and reconstructed it to the proto-language. It appears in a limited number of recurring patterns with specific functions throughout the family, and interacts with the rest of Dravidian grammar in a simple and direct manner. General schemas have been proposed for the analysis of the SVF in its synchronic and diachronic aspects. These contributions represent in and of themselves a significant advance over previous study, which has for the most part failed to perceive the systematic importance of the SVF for Dravidian grammar. But when put in proper perspective, the distance we have come in pursuit of the SVF falls far short of the distance we still have to go. Our re-evaluation of existing work and exploration of the new must continue with an enhanced understanding of the SVF and its role in general Dravidian grammar.

The study of three areas where morphology and syntax interact will cast new light on our knowledge about the SVF in particular, and comparative Dravidian grammar in general: agreement, finiteness, and the structure of complex sentences. Agreement is a morphological means of interpreting finiteness, but is poorly understood in the daughter languages. Various kinds of agreement, it has been suggested, arise from the application of such diverse rules as subject-predicate agreement, Rule (45), Reduplication, and Echo Compound Formation. In none of the daughter languages have the conditions on these rules been satisfactorily formulated. Finiteness is a crucial syntactic parameter of the Dravidian sentence, but is commonly regarded as little more than a morphological exponent of the class of verbs. It helps to define the relation of a construction to its head at the level of the sentence (functional finiteness) and below it (formal finiteness). Yet, studies of Dravidian syntax fail to mention the contribution of finiteness. Moreover, the structure of the sentence and its constituents, some of which embed the SVF, is largely unexplored territory. Intensive study of the grammar of complex sentences should greatly enhance our knowledge of the role that finiteness plays in their formation, and consequently improve our analysis of the SVF.

Extensive analysis of the SVF is needed in the individual daughter languages, particularly the classical and non-literary languages. As Chapter

IV indicates, the study of individual branches such as the south-central subgroup may prove to be enormously rewarding. These studies would in turn contribute to the reconstruction of Proto-Dravidian. This would ultimately enable us to determine the role and source of the SVF in the South Asian linguistic area, so that the appearance of the SVF in an Indo-Aryan language like Marathi might be attributed to the influence of Dravidian, and not the other way around.

Our analysis of the SVF in the Dravidian languages may stimulate research in the history of linguistics, language typology, and the principles governing the interaction of morphology and syntax. Our analysis of the concept of a formally finite verb can be taken as a reconstruction of the traditional Tamil grammarians' term *muṟṟeccam*. Further study of this tradition will not only help antiquarians to reconstruct the traditional concepts that might underly Rule (103), but also show contemporary linguists how a school of grammatical analysis based on lexical and morphological primes can handle syntactic description. Typologists may wish to compare the Dravidian system of agreement with those found in other language families. It is suggestive that many Western grammarians point to the lack of agreement between adjectives and nouns in Dravidian, but never draw attention to the agreement among the components of a SVF. These studies may ultimately cast new light on the role of finiteness in co-ordinating the morphological and syntactic dimensions of sentence structure; and in doing so, persuade syntacticians to add finiteness to their arsenal of descriptive devices and their theoretical debates.

NOTES

Chapter One

FINITENESS AND THE DRAVIDIAN SENTENCE

1. Krishnamurti's (1978: 2) subgrouping of the Dravidian languages is assumed throughout: South Dravidian: Tamil, Malayāḷam, Iruḷa, Kota, Toda, Koḍagu, Kannaḍa, Tulu; South-Central Dravidian: Telugu, Gonḍi, Konḍa, Pengo, Manḍa, Kūi, Kūvi; Central Dravidian: Kolami, Parji, Ollari (also Koṇekor Gadaba), Naiki, Gadaba; North Dravidian: Malto, Kuṛux (also Dhangar), Brahui.
2. This use of the term serial verb differs from the one that is commonly found in the literature on South Asian languages, where it generally refers to any compound verb formation that uses participles, gerunds, or infinitives. No misunderstanding should arise if this is borne in mind.
3. This definition appears in the text because it describes the most common finite verb forms in the Dravidian languages, but not all of them. A revision should make provisions to include all of the personal verb forms in a given language, whether or not they encode tense. The conjugated negative verb form in Old Tamil, e.g. *kāṇēṉ* 'I do not see' is finite even though it does not mark tense. The contingent verb in Kannaḍa, e.g. *bandānu* '(lest) he might come' is also a finite verb even though it encodes modality, not tense. Thus, any personal verb form is a finite verb, regardless of whether it additionally incorporates a morpheme for tense, negation, or modality. Tense appears in this definition because it is the verbal category that finite verbs most commonly encode. For example, while a finite verb form that incorporates a morpheme for negation or modality always entails the existence of a finite form that incorporates a morpheme for tense, the reverse is not true. The definition must make reference to some verbal category in order to distinguish finite verb forms from predicate nominals that are inflected for subject-predicate agreement, e.g. Old Tamil *nāṭṭēṉ* 'I am a countryman', so it mentions tense as the most salient verbal category.
4. Bloomfield (1933: 267), for example, treats finiteness as a syntactic property that inheres in the actor-action construction in English.
5. Imperative verb forms do distinguish between a singular and a plural form, and may be said to incorporate reference to the second person by virtue of co-occurring with second person pronouns.
6. Some attempt to overcome this problem and assimilate these different speech-act verb forms to ordinary finite verb forms by combining them to create a single "imperative" paradigm. In such a paradigm, the hortative appears in the first person, the imperative in the second person, and the optative and permissive in the third person. They can then be said to incorporate subject-verb agreement markers by virtue of their mutual contrast in a single paradigm.

   The defective morphology of some modals may be traced to their use as verbs that express a speech-act, e.g., the negative imperative in Modern Kannaḍa is expressed by combining the modal auxiliary verb *bēḍa* 'must not' with the infinitive of the main verb. Such verbs tend to occur exclusively in root clauses, and to lose what non- finite forms they might have had.

7. The categories that subject-verb agreement markers encode are not verbal categories, but nominal categories such as person, number, and gender, all of which characterize the participants in either the narrated event or the speech event. It therefore comes as no surprise that these agreement markers also appear on predicate nominals in a number of Dravidian languages, e.g. Old Tamil, Goṇḍi.
8. The syntactic definition makes the loss of subject-verb agreement markers in Malayāḷam look less catastrophic than it does on the morphological definition. On the syntactic definition, Modern Malayāḷam has finite verb forms; on the morphological definition, it does not.
9. We consider below a small class of sentences in which a non-finite verb form such as the infinitive appears in the specially designated position for finite predicates to convey a speech-act.
10. In the theoretical paradigm of these authors there is a solution to the problem posed by the existence of sentences with predicate nominals. Such sentences could be derived from sentences with a copular verb such as *ā- 'become' (*DEDR* 333), which is conventionally "elided" or, in modern terms, deleted. The two kinds of sentences differ semantically: a sentence with a predicate nominal generally predicates an essential property of the subject, while one with the copula *ā- 'become' generally predicates an accidental property. To the extent that such differences exist, the one cannot be derived from the other.
11. These conditions are insufficient to interpret the finiteness of an auxiliary compound verb in a root clause. Steever (1983) argues that the main and auxiliary verbs in such a compound c-command each other. He provides an algorithm to permit the proper interpretation of finiteness in such cases. For the most part, however, the condition that the finite predicate appear at the extreme right boundary of the sentence is sufficient because auxiliary verbs appear to the right of their main verbs.
12. The morphological interpretation of finiteness varies from language to language, according to the morphological potentials of the word-class to which the finite predicate belongs. This calls for a variable definition of morphological finiteness, one which may be developed along the following lines. A predicate is finite if it marks the maximum number of grammatical categories with which it is endowed by the word-class to which it belongs, and, in the case of defective forms, by the details of its lexical entry. The presence of personal endings on a predicate is a good indicator that the predicate is finite, because personal endings generally imply the presence of other grammatical categories, but the other categories do not imply the presence of personal endings. Thus, a form with a personal ending generally encodes the maximum number of categories provided by the word-class to which it belongs. Aside from Malayāḷam, verbs are morphologically finite if they mark subject-predicate agreement and a verbal category such as tense, negation, or modality. Hence, verbs that marked one of these verbal categories but not subject-verb agreement would not be finite. This would not apply in Malayāḷam where the verb morphology does not provide personal endings. Similarly, in some languages predicate nominals indicate their finiteness with subject-predicate agreement markers, but in others, where the appropriate morphology is lacking, they cannot. A predicate nominal that marks the category of person always implies the existence of one that marks number and, perhaps, gender, but the reverse is not true.
13. See note 11. To assign finiteness properly to an auxiliary compound verb in a root clause, only precedence relations are needed.
14. Andronov (1970: 53) lists upwards of ten parts of speech for Tamil. But they can be analyzed as combinations of nouns and verbs. For example, the so-called adverb *ippoẓutu* 'now' is a noun-noun compound that consists of *i-* 'this (one)' and *poẓutu*

'time, sun'. The so-called adverb *cikkiramāka* 'quickly, urgently' consists of the noun *cikkiram* 'urgency' and the verb *āka* 'become, serve a role'.

15. The reconstruction of the grammatical, or abstract cases such as the nominative, accusative, dative, and genitive is more certain than the reconstruction of the localistic, or concrete cases such as the locative and ablative. The evolution of the localistic cases is marked by frequcnt replacement with locative postpositions.

16. Here I wish to include, contrary to tradition, verbal nouns. I treat them as relative participles that combine with a pronominal head, instead of a full lexical noun.

17. The theory of case thus prevents the use of a case-marker to combine the two Tamil simple sentences (i) and (ii) into a complex sentence in (iii), even though there is no obvious semantic reason to bar this use. The dative case (*-ukku*) is commonly used to mark the direct object of a verb of fearing, while the instrumental case (*-āl*) is often used to identify the proximate cause of an action. But the theory of case constrains these syntactic and semantic considerations so that they apply only within a single clause, hence (iii) is ungrammatical.

(i) *avaḷ* *añc-iṉ-āḷ.*
she-nom fear-pst-3sf
'She was afraid.'

(ii) *avaṉ* *keṭṭa* *paiyaṉ.*
he-nom bad boy-nom
'He is a bad boy.'

(iii) **avaḷ* *avaṉ* *keṭṭa* *paiyaṉ-āl/-ukku* *añc-iṉ-āḷ.*
she-nom he-nom bad boy-instr/-dat fear-pst-3sf
'She was afraid because he is a bad boy.'

18. It is also possible that some sentences have a subject inflected for the locative case or some locative postposition. Possible examples include the Kannaḍa *nanna-hattira haṇa ide* 'I$_1$ have$_3$ money$_2$' (lit. 'money$_1$ is$_3$ near-me$_2$', and the Kuṛux *abṛar-nu jhagṛa manja kera* 'they$_1$ have$_4$ gotten$_3$ into a quarrel$_2$' (lit. 'a quarrel$_2$ has$_4$ occurred$_3$ among-them$_1$'. It is not yet clear whether these locative subjects have the subject-coding properties that nominative and dative subjects do, e.g. the ability to trigger Reflexivization (allative datives cannot). This does not affect our overall analysis of simple sentences.

19. The descriptive adequacy of Rule (1) can also be tested against simple sentences with compound verb formations, which will tend to confirm it. We must however dispense with their evidence here because their proper analysis would lead us too far afield of our primary task. See note 11.

20. The morphological definition of *viṉaiyeccam* as a 'verb that anticipates a following verb' must be replaced by a syntactic definition according to which it is interpreted as a 'verb that anticipates a following predicate'. This change is necessary to accommodate examples such as (11)c. The definition of *peyareccam* as a 'verb that anticipates a following noun' must also be replaced by a syntactic definition according to which it is interpreted as a 'verb that anticipates a following nominal expression'. This change accommodates verbal nouns which may be viewed as a combination of an adnominal participle and a pronominal head.

21. To the best of my knowledge, the use of the conjunctive participle to mark a subordinate clause governed by a verb of perception is an indepedent development within Tamil. Other languages such as Telugu would have a verbal noun inflected for the accusative case in place of the conjunctive participle in such a construction (Tamil also has this variant).

22. In fact, a variant of this formula substitutes verbal nouns, *pōvatu* 'going' in literary Tamil and *pōkiratu* 'ibid' in the spoken language, for the infinitive *pōka* 'go'. Verbal nouns are in this context interpreted as finite predicate nominals.

23. Similarly, some languages permit the substitution of the non-finite conditional form with the finite imperative to form a supposition. See example (60)b.

24. In some languages such as Toda and Parji the distinction between the adnominal participle and certain verbal nouns seems to have been neutralized in favor of what historically was the latter. In such languages the relative clause is a noun-noun compound in which the first noun is the verbal noun and the second the head noun.

Chapter Two

MULTIPLE FINITE PREDICATES

1. The presence of these verbs in a structure, either through base generation or transformational insertion, changes the expression it combines with into a derived or pseudo-direct object. Since such expressions should be morphologically interpreted by the theory of case-marking, they are immune to the effects of Rule (1). Thus, Rule (1) is structurally dependent to this extent, not global, in its application.
2. The semantic interpretation of some sentences includes the lexical contribution of **ā-* 'become' and **en-* 'say, think'; but in others, it is ignored. This corresponds roughly to the distinction between base-generation and transformational insertion of these lexemes. The insertion of these verbs is motivated by their syntactic properties, viz. the ability to embed finite predicates.
3. See note 2. It is this unique property that leads to the transformational insertion of these verbs into a structure to preserve a finite predicate in a dependent clause.
4. These verbs are polypersonal: they incorporate the transition particle (tp) which signals agreement with a first or second person direct or indirect object. See Steever (1979).
5. This example contains an instance of a serial verb, which is discussed at greater length below in Chapter Five under the section on the present perfect tense in Parji.
6. Some verbs in Koṇḍa have truncated personal endings, which descend from full ending in pre-Koṇḍa. They are indicative of serial verbs, and are discussed in Chapter Four.
7. Proto-Dravidian **-ō* 'or, whether' has become *-o* in Koṇḍa in the wake of a far-reaching phonological change that has neutralized the distinction between short and long vowels in the non-initial syllables of simple words. This development is carried further in Goṇḍi (see below) where length is no longer phonemic.
8. Compare this with the Kūi tag-question marker *gina* 'isn't it so?' from Indo-Aryan *ki* 'or' and the Dravidian interrogative particle *-ā* (with an epenthetic *-n-*).

Chapter Three

SERIAL VERBS IN SOUTH DRAVIDIAN

1. An attempt might be made to assimilate the two agreement rules. This is done by inserting an inflected form of the verb *ā-* 'become' into sentences with predicate nominals, from which the personal ending would be copied onto the predicate nominal. However, in the affirmative the presence versus absence of *ā-* is correlated with a semantic distinction between accidental and essential qualities. This difference seems to be neutralized in the negative where the verb *al-* 'not become' appears in both cases. Its insertion into sentences that use a predicate nominal to predicate an essential property of its subject probably follows from the fact that the

negative morpheme must be realized in a verb form. The verb *al-* is chosen because its insertion will least disturb the morphology and syntax of the host sentence. But the semantic distinction in the positive prevents the identification of the two agreement rules for the time being.

2. The revision of Rule (44) should retain the term 'functionally finite predicate' even if Rule (45) is absent. This allows for the possibility of SVFs generated by means other than Rule (45), such as *ki*-Echo Formation (see below). It also acknowledges the precedence of the functional over the formal characterization of finiteness.
3. However, sectarian *bhakti* literature may include the echo compound in its arsenal of polemic devices. Writing in Kannaḍa in the tenth century, the *vīraśaiva* saint *basavaṇṇa* employed the echo compound to ridicule non-*śaiva* deities such as *Nārāyaṇa* (a form of *Viṣṇu*) and *Bomma* (Kannaḍa *tadbhava* of *Brahma*). The two examples are the first two lines of *vacana* 550.

(i) *nārāyaṇan* *embavana* *kāṇe* *gīrāyaṇan* *embavana* *kāṇe*
Narayana-nom say-vn-acc see-neg-1s *gi*-nom say-vn-acc see-neg-1s
'I acknowledge no one called Nārāyaṇa, called Shmārāyaṇa.'

(ii) *bomman* *embavana* *kāṇe* *gimman* *embavana* *kāṇe*
Bomma-nom say-vn-acc see-neg-1s *gi*-nom say-vn-acc see-neg-1s
'I acknowledge no one called Bomma, called Shmomma.'

4. Since *ki*-echo compounds involve quantification, it might be proposed to treat them as a kind of FPEC which is realized through reduplication rather than the cliticization of a particle. However, *ki*-echo formation creates a lexical compound, and does not embed a sentence. It may be that in both cases quantification permits the occurrence of a finite predicate with each surface manifestation of the quantifier. Why this is so must be answered in future research.
5. This recalls Adjukiewicz' categorial grammar, which has become an integral part of model-theoretic semantics. However, the combinatoric properties of *eccam* are firmly grounded in morphological categories, not logical ones.
6. In stating word-formation rules the following conventions are used: *X* : *Y*, *X is rewritten as Y* and *Anything with the form of Y is a X*; *VB*, verb base; *Neg*, negative; *Pst Tns*, past tense; *PE*, personal ending; *PE*[1]...*PE*[1], discontinuous personal ending; *Tns*[1]...*Tns*[1], discontinuous tense marker.
7. In Tamil and Kannaḍa, the past tense form can be used to signal certain performance of an action in the immediate future.

Chapter Four

SERIAL VERBS IN SOUTH-CENTRAL DRAVIDIAN

1. This replacement of the personal forms of *kā-* 'not become' with the invariant form *kādu* 'it does not become' compromises the analysis of these forms as SVFs since the agreement features of the two component parts are no longer identical. However, the third person singular neuter form of the paradigm is the least marked, and therefore referentially includes all the more marked members of the paradigm. See Steever 1981, Chapter 4.
2. Affix-Truncation may in fact be generalized from its present form so that it applies in any compound verb whose head marks tense, regardless of whether it is finite or not. In its generalized form it would apply in compound verbs when the head had the form of the adnominal participle or the conditional: both verbs mark tense, but not subject-verb agreement. As the application of Affix-Truncation expands to

include more kinds of verbs, it loses its purely morphological character and begins to assume a phonological one. For more examples of compound verbs whose parts show agreement with non-finite inflections, see the Kuṛux examples in (91) in Chapter VI. The rule of Affix-Truncation is retained in this specific form to aid comparison with certain constructions in Pengo and Kolami below. These data suggest that this rule originally applied only to finite verb forms, so that its application to non-finite forms in Koṇḍa is an innovation.

3. Whether or not a structure derives from a complex sentence in underlying structure does not materially affect its interpretation as a SVF or not. Rule (44) is really a constraint on the surface distribution of finite predicates.
4. The rule of Auxiliary Verb Deletion, as it applies to the Koṇḍa auxiliary verb *ā-* 'become', and only to this auxiliary, can be replaced by two phonological rules that are independently required in Koṇḍa grammar (Steever 1987). They are Vowel Shortening and Vowel Cluster Deletion. Vowel Shortening is a pervasive phonological process in all South-Central Dravidian languages except Telugu and Goṇḍi that neutralizes the distinction between long and short vowels in non-initial syllables in favor of the short. Once Auxiliary Contraction has applied in Chart 1, the long vowel of the auxiliary *ā-* 'become' occurs in a non-initial syllable and is accordingly shortened. The process of Vowel Cluster Deletion transforms diphthongs into monophthongs in Koṇḍa: a phonotactic constraint prohibits the direct conjunction of two vowels. Once Affix-Truncation applies in Chart 1, the vowel of the truncated personal ending and the shortened vowel of the auxiliary *ā-* 'become' come into contact, triggering the application of Vowel Cluster Deletion which replaces the sequence *-V-a-* with *-V-*. The rule of Auxiliary Verb Deletion is retained as shorthand for these two processes in Koṇḍa, and to aid comparison with similar examples of contraction, e.g. the Pengo present perfect. These phonological processes cannot be invoked in other languages to replace Auxiliary Verb Deletion.
5. The personal endings each have several allomorphs, whose presence is governed by a variety of conditions. The allomorphs with a short vowel appear on the synthetic present perfect, while those with a long vowel appear on the simple past tense form in Classical Tamil. The modern language has eliminated most of this allomorphic variation, so that the synthetic present perfect in Sri Lankan Tamil has now assumed the allomorphs with a long vowel. Nothing in our argument for the etymology of the synthetic present perfect depends crucially on this.
6. Auxiliary Verb Deletion, as it applies to the perfect tense auxiliary *man* 'be', varies from language to language with respect to how much of the auxiliary's lexical base can be deleted. In Kūvi, for example, the reduced form of *man* is *mn*. It should therefore come as no surprise that only part of the lexical base is deleted in the present instance.

Chapter Seven

THE SERIAL VERB FORMATION IN DRAVIDIAN SYNTAX

1. The claim made here is that the systematic and comparative importance of the SVF has been overlooked. The individual authors have recorded the SVF in the various languages, often included in the texts without any further discussion. (Krishnamurti 1969: 304, pass. is the only author to discuss the construction at length.) Indeed, this book could not exist without these descriptions.

2. As before, the category of tense is used as an abbreviation for the set of verbal categories including tense, negation, and mood. See note 3, Chapter I.
3. Some similarity may exist between the two kinds of finiteness. The variety that applies to the SVF may take *V*'' as its domain, while the variety that applies to the subject-predicate relation may take *V*''' as its domain, where *V*''' is equivalent to *S*. Assimilation of the two may not be readily made, however, because the former is an example of dependent-marking in Nichols' (1986) sense; the latter, an example of head-marking.

BIBLIOGRAPHY

IJDL—International Journal of Dravidian Linguistics
JAOS—Journal of the American Oriental Society
Lg—Language

ADJUKIEWICZ, K. 1935. Die syntaktische Konexität. *Studia Philosophia* vol. I, pp. 1-27.

AGESTHIALINGOM, S. 1983. Historical linguistics and generative grammar. Paper presented at the National Seminar on Language Variation and Language Change, January 6-7, 1983. Hyderabad: Department of Linguistics, Osmania University.

akkamahādevi, 1977. *akkana vacanagaḷu*. Edited by L. Basavaraju. Mysore: Gita Book House.

ANDRES, SUSIE. 1977. A description of Muria Goṇḍi phonology and morphology with a transformational account of the morphophonological processes employed. Unpublished Ph. D. dissertation. Poona: Deccan College Postgraduate and Research Institute. (Available from University Microfilms, Ann Arbor and London.)

ANDRONOV, MICHAEL. 1970. *Dravidian Languages.* Moscow: Nauka Publishing House.

ARDEN, A. H. 1937. *A progressive grammar of the Telugu language*. Madras: Christian Literature Society.

basavaṇṇa. 1979. *basavaṇṇavara ṭikina vacanagalu*. Edited by M. M. Kalaburgi. Dharwar: Kannaḍa Adhyayana Pīṭha, Karnāṭaka Viśvavidyālaya

BENVENISTE, EMILE. 1965. Structure des rélations d'auxiliarité. *Acta Linguistica Hafniensia* 9, pp. 1-15.

BHATTACHARYA, S. 1956. *Ollari, a Dravidian speech*. Calcutta: Anthropological Survey of India.

BHASKARARAO, PERI. 1977. *Reduplication and onomatopoeia in Telugu*. Poona: Deccan College Postgraduate and Research Institute.

————. 1980. *Koṇekor Gadaba, a Dravidian language*. Pune: Deccan College Postgraduate and Research Institute.

BLOCH, JULES. 1946. *Structure grammaticale des langues dravidiennes*. Paris: Adrien-Maisonneuve.

BLOOMFIELD, LEONARD. 1933. *Language*. New York: Holt, Rinehart and Winston. Reprinted 1975. Delhi: Motilal Banarsidass.

BRAY, DENYS. 1901. *The Brahui language, Part I—Introduction and grammar*. Calcutta.

BRIGHT, WILLIAM. 1958. *An outline of colloquial Kannada*. Poona: Deccan College Postgraduate and Research Institute.

BURROW, THOMAS AND S. BHATTACHARYA. 1953. *The Parji language: a Dravidian language of Bastar*. Hertford: Stephen Austin and Sons, Ltd.

————. 1970. *The Pengo language: Grammar texts, and vocabulary*, Oxford: Clarendon Press.

BURROW, THOMAS AND MURRAY B. EMENEAU. 1984. *A Dravidian etymological dictionary, 2nd edition*. Oxford: Clarendon Press.

CALDWELL, ROBERT. 1856. *A comparative grammar of the Dravidian or South-Indian family of languages*, 1st edition, London; 3rd edition, revised by J. L. Wyatt and T. Ramakrishna Pillai, London, 1913 (reprinted in 1976 by University of Madras Press, Madras).

DAS, A. SISIR KUMAR. 1973. *Structure of Malto*. Annamalainagar: Annamalai University.

DROESE, ERNEST. 1884. *Introduction to the Malto language*. Agra: Secundara Orphanage Press.

EKKA, FRANCIS. 1971. A grammar of Kụ̄rux language. Unpublished Ph. D. dissertation. Madurai: Madurai Kamaraj University.

———. 1979. Some aspects of Kūṛux aspect. *IJDL* 8, pp. 277-84.

EMENEAU, MURRAY B. 1938a. Echo-words in Toda. *New Indian Antiquary* 1, pp. 98-112.

———. 1938b. An echo-word motif in Dravidian folk-tales. *JAOS* 58, pp. 553-70.

———. 1939. Another example of the echo-word motif in Dravidian folktales. *JAOS* 59, pp. 503-505.

———. 1944-46. *Kota texts.* University of California Publications in Linguistics, vols. 2 and 3. Berkeley: University of California Press.

———. 1955. *Kolami, a Dravidian language.* University of California Publications in Linguistics, vol. 12. Berkeley: University of California Press.

———. 1980. *Language and linguistic area.* Edited by Anwar S. Dil. Stanford: Stanford University Press.

———. 1984. *Toda grammar and texts.* American Philosophical Society, Memoirs series 155. Philadelphia: American Philosophical Society.

GAIR, JAMES AND S. SUSEENDIRARAJAH. 1981. Some aspects of the Jaffna Tamil verbal system. *IJDL* 10, pp. 37-84.

GORDON, KENT. Clause patterns in Dhangar-Kurux. In Ronald Trail (ed.), *Patterns in clause, sentence, and discourse in selected languages of India and Nepal.* Norman Oklahoma: Summer Institute of Linguistics.

HAHN, FREDERICK. 1911. *Kurukh grammar.* Calcutta.

ISRAEL, MICHAEL. 1979. *A grammar of the Kūvi language.* Trivandrum: Dravidian Linguistics Association.

KRISHNAMURTI, BH. 1969, *Koṇḍa or Kūbi, a Dravidian language.* Hyderabad: Tribal Culture Research and Training Institute.

———. 1978. Areal and lexical diffusion of sound change. *Lg* 54, no. 1, pp. 1-20.

KRISHNAMURTI, BH. AND J. GWYNN. 1985. *A grammar of modern Telugu.* Delhi: Oxford India.

KURYLOWICZ, JERZY. 1964. *The inflectional categories of Indo-European.* Heidelberg : Carl Winter.

LAKOFF, GEORGE. 1970. *Irregularity in syntax.* New York: Holt, Rinehart and Winston.

LAKSHMI BAI. 1985. Some notes on correlative constructions in Dravidian. In Veneeta Acson and Richard Land (eds.), *For Gordon Fairbanks.* Honolulu: University of Hawaii Press.

MAHAPATRA, B. P. 1979. *Malto—an ethnosemantic study.* Mysore: Central Institute of Indian Languages.

NICHOLS, JOHANNA. 1986. Head-marking and dependent-marking grammar. *Lg.* 62, no. 1, pp. 56-119.

PARAMASIVAM, K. 1979. *Effectivity and causativity in Tamil.* Trivandrum: Dravidian Linguistics Association.

PERLMUTTER, DAVID. 1971. *Deep and surface structure constraints in syntax.* New York: Holt, Rinehart and Winston.

RAMASAMI, K. 1981. Correlative relative clauses in Tamil. In S. Agesthialingom and N. Rajasekharan Nair (eds.), *Dravidian syntax,* pp. 363-80. Annamalainagar: Annamalai University.

SEUREN, PIETER. 1969. *Operators and nucleus, a contribution to the theory of grammar.* Cambridge: Cambridge University Press.

SHANMUGAM, S. V. 1971. *Dravidian nouns, a comparative study.* Annamalainagar: Annamalai University.

SPENCER, HAROLD. 1985. *A Kannada grammar.* New Delhi: Asian Educational Services.

SRIDHAR, S. N. 1987. *Kannada.* London: Croom Held Ltd.

STEEVER, SANFORD B. 1979. The genesis of polypersonal verbs in South-Central Dravidian. *IJDL* 9, pp. 337-73.

———. 1981. *Selected papers in Tamil and Dravidian linguistics*. Madurai: Muttu Patippakam.

———. 1983. A study in auxiliation: the grammar of the indicative auxiliary verb system of Tamil. Unpublished Ph. D. dissertation. Chicago: Department of Linguistics, University of Chicago.

———. 1984. The evolution of the present perfect in Pengo. *JAOS* 104, pp. 621-48.

———. 1987. The origins of the past negative in Konda. *JAOS* 107, pp. 71-80.

SUBRAHMANYAM, P. S. 1968. *A descriptive grammar of Gondi*. Annamalainagar: Annamalai University.

———. 1971. *Dravidian verbal morphology*. Annamalainagar: Annamalai University.

tolkāppiyam collaitikāram. 1974. (With *cēṉāvaraiyar*'s commentary.) Tinevely: South Indian Saiva Siddhanta Publishtng House.

VEPSER, DON. 1971. Kurukh syntax with special reference to the verbal system. Unpublished Ph. D. dissertation. Chicago: Department of Linguistics, University of Chicago.

WINFIELD, W.W. 1928. *A grammar of the Kūi language*. Calcutta: Baptist Mission Press.

ZVELEBIL, KAMIL. 1977. *A sketch of comparative Dravidian morphology, part one*. The Hague: Mouton & Co.

[illegible]

INDEX